unMothered, unTongued

The Sue William Silverman Prize for Creative Nonfiction

unMothered, unTongued

Lyric Essays

Lee Horikoshi Roripaugh

Selected by Chloé Cooper Jones

The University of Georgia Press ATHENS

This book is the winner of the 2024 Sue William Silverman Prize for Creative Nonfiction, part of the Association of Writers & Writing Programs (AWP) Award Series. AWP is a nonprofit organization dedicated to amplifying the voices of writers and the academic programs and organizations that serve them. Please visit www.awpwriter.org for more information.

Published by the University of Georgia Press
Athens, Georgia 30602
www.ugapress.org

Designed by Erin Kirk
Set in Adobe Garamond Pro and Whitney
Printed and bound by Sheridan Books, Inc.
The paper in this book meets the guidelines for permanence and durability of the Committee on Production Guidelines for Book Longevity of the Council on Library Resources.

Most University of Georgia Press titles are available from popular e-book vendors.

EU Authorized Representative
Easy Access System Europe—Mustamäe tee 50, 10621
Tallinn, Estonia, gpsr.requests@easproject.com

Printed in the United States of America
29 28 27 26 25 P 5 4 3 2 1

Library of Congress Cataloging-in-Publication Data

Names: Roripaugh, Lee Ann, author. | Cooper Jones, Chloé, 1983– editor.
Title: unMothered, unTongued : lyric essays / Lee Horikoshi Roripaugh ; selected by Chloé Cooper Jones.
Description: Athens : The University of Georgia Press, [2025] | Series: The Sue William Silverman Prize for creative nonfiction
Identifiers: LCCN 2025007461 | ISBN 9780820374413 (paperback) | ISBN 9780820374420 (epub) | ISBN 9780820374437 (pdf)
Subjects: LCSH: Roripaugh, Lee Ann. | Japanese Americans—West (U.S.)—Biography. | Poets, American—Biography. | Identity (Philosophical concept) | American essays—21st century.
Classification: LCC PS3568.O717 U56 2025 | DDC 814/.54 [B]—dc23/eng/20250508
LC record available at https://lccn.loc.gov/2025007461

Contents

unMothered, unTongued

Motherlands and Mother Tongues

Five Reflections on Language and Landscape

1. I Want to Be a Cowboy / And You Can Be My Cowgirl

Of course, you want to be a cowboy. You have a cowboy hat, a brown plaid Western shirt with snap buttons, Lee blue jeans with a leather belt hand tooled for you by your American grandfather, and sometimes you're allowed to wear one of your father's bolo ties. Dressed as a cowboy, you are gender ambiguous. It is one of your favorite outfits.

Of course, you want to be a cowboy. You want to ride broncos in the rodeo like your father did when he was young, bottle-feed orphaned sheep at the ranch your American grandparents used to own outside Lander, Wyoming, shoot rattlesnakes in their apple orchard. You wield your father's toy pistols from when he was a boy—in love with their realistic detailing and sinister heft—although you're forbidden to play with them outside. In the backyard of your parents' house, in Laramie, Wyoming, the Caragana trees snap and explode their seed pods in late August like cap guns, and you're an outlaw crouching behind the Nanking cherry trees, fending off a hail of bullets. Inside, your father's manual Olivetti studio typewriter sounds like distant artillery fire.

Of course, you want to be a cowboy, but with your thick dark hair, inherited from your Japanese mother, and your ambiguous, biracial features, you are always, instead, the default "Indian" in playground games with other children. In elementary school, at Thanksgiving, you are never, ever a pilgrim. Each year, it somehow becomes obligatory that you wear your hair in braids and don a construction paper headband with an Elmer's-glued-on feather. It's not so much that you don't *want* to be an "Indian," but rather the unspoken *impossibility* of your ever being a pilgrim—or a cowboy, which of course you *want* to be—that troubles you. It's through these gestures of obligatory categorization and exclusion that your tenuous state of never quite *belonging to* or *belonging in* the American West is constantly made apparent to you.

Because *cowboy*, as fantasy space, is a space of privilege you'll never occupy: white, straight, male, someone who feels *entitled* to confidently *occupy* the American West. Perhaps this American pipe dream is a macrocosm of the abusive household in which you grow up—where, all evidence to the contrary, you're ruthlessly expected, through a combination of parental narcissism and performative contortions of American exceptionalism, to occupy the center. Where, although academically and musically gifted, you're also painfully shy, painfully sensitive, painfully strange. Where your parents attempt to shame and beat the shyness, the sensitivity, the strangeness out of you. Where, despite the giftedness, you're constantly made to feel like a colossal disappointment. Where, if you fail to comply, in even the smallest way, with your parents' scripting, you're accused of being a "bad seed," a "troublemaker," and you are punished.

You, as your "self's self," are never enough. Which is probably why you think you want to be a cowboy.

2. Snapshots

Cowboy is not the only mask you don however. Your childhood pictures show you wearing multiple costumes, in a bizarre array of highly stylized poses: prancing jazz-handed baton twirler in a pink checked dress and a white headband, sailor-suited sailor, professor wearing your father's mortarboard contemplating a copy of *Winnie the Pooh*, ballerina in a yellow tutu assuming the dying swan pose. Most of the pictures are taken on top of the dining room table, cleared off to function as a makeshift stage. The photo shoots are lengthy, tedious, and there's much poking, prodding, and primping. Your father goes through rolls of film. Your mother choreographs these photo sessions with the grim determination of a drill sergeant. The psychotically perky poses she insists you assume are obviously culled from vintage midcentury children's sweater pattern booklets such as Clark, Spinnerin, and Bernat—featuring well-groomed, well-mannered, dimpled and doe-eyed, wholesome *white* children. Your mother consults these booklets with intense concentration, along with a book in Japanese she owns called *The American Way of Housekeeping*, seemingly as guidebooks for assimilation.

Your mother is big on coaching. Before taking you to tea parties, she drills you beforehand, asking you potential questions, to which you deliver the memorized answers she's provided for you ahead of time—answers occasionally accompanied by coquettish physical gestures she's devised. (When wearing the cowboy outfit, for example, if someone asks your name, you're supposed to turn around, one hand on outthrust hip in reference to the leather tag on your jeans, and exclaim, *Lee*! If someone asks what your father does, you're supposed to reply, *My father's an Arthur!* It's supposed to be *author*, but sometimes things get confused in between your mother's accent and the limitations of your own budding vocabulary.)

And so rather than being spontaneous or candid, family picture taking's always a highly performative, formal—and possibly somewhat Japanese?—affair. Your mother is tense and critical, while you sulk in cranky boredom. But of course, there's much more at stake for your mother than the mere capturing of snapshots. In retrospect, you think she's clearly *fashioning* and *manufacturing* images—images intended to represent her own Americanness, or perhaps more importantly, *your* Americanness. When you think about these snapshots, you're reminded of the underlying sense of strain, the feeling that making these images is terribly difficult work, that they are a product of trying too hard, that the *deliberation* that goes behind all the costuming, choreographing, and posing—rather than capturing the 1950's wholesome Americana your mother seems to be insistently striving for—reveals instead the tricky and unspoken cultural fault lines underlying your parents' miscegenated marriage. (It is Laramie, Wyoming, early 1970s. It is post–World War II, post–Korean War. The Vietnam War flickers in menacing black-and-white footage on the television.)

As if this weren't enough, these images have to pass muster on two continents, for these are the pictures your mother also sends to her father, your Japanese grandfather, as representation and validation for the life she has chosen—with a "Yankee," no less—in America.

But still . . . where *are* you—indeed, *who* are you—in these snapshots, underneath these costumes, behind these masks?

3. Good Lee Hunting

Your father teaches you how to shoot: shotgun, rifle, handgun. In the fall, he takes you hunting: dove, sage grouse, antelope. You use the rifle and shotgun that belonged to your American grandmother, with a shortened stock for smaller arms, and your father makes cross sticks to steady your rifle when hunting antelope at long distance through a telescope. You are an extremely sensitive child, but you like to shoot, and you're fascinated by the biology of the gutting, the skinning, the dressing.

Your American grandfather taught your father to shoot and took him hunting, and now your father has taught you to shoot and takes you hunting. You don't want to be a girl or a "sissy" about this. You want to please your father, make him proud. You're troubled by the killing, but there's still a small part of you that's secretly pleased. Even in Wyoming, most of the girls in your junior high or high school classes typically don't go hunting with their fathers or brothers. Every fall, your father takes pictures of you in your safety orange hat and vest with your shotgun and your sage grouse or your rifle and your antelope. It is a rite of passage. There are trophies. It is vaguely Hemingway-esque. One year, drunk hunters swing by in their truck to admire your downed buck, and when they get close enough to see your braids sticking out from under your hat, they yell, *Goddamn, it's a girl!*

Your father is a writer. You frequently fall asleep to the explosive clattering of your father's manual typewriter in the dining room as he writes late into the night. A novelist, short story writer, and poet, he will eventually become the state poet laureate of Wyoming, and he refers to himself as a *cowboy poet.* Of course, you want to be a cowboy poet too. Whenever your father publishes a poem, he puts it on the refrigerator with a magnet, and so you ask to have your crayoned drawings magnetized to the fridge as well. Soon you are obsessively writing—journals, poems, stories—and eventually your father lets you use one of his castoff manual typewriters.

Your father writes and teaches Western literature. His novels, stories, and poems deal with Wyoming ranch life, as well as the culture and landscape of the American West. In the same way you intuitively understand the element of gender and racial transgression inherent in shooting and hunting with your father, you also intuitively understand the element of gender and racial transgression inherent in your writing. Or maybe what you mean by this is that you intuitively understand that to write as your father writes, about the things your father writes about, is to write within a certain Western literary tradition, and from a subject position that is typically male and typically white. It's not that you're not given female authors and poets to read—because you are—or that you're not given writers of color to read—because, once again, you are—but rather that you have no available literary mirror to reflect or speak to your jumbled nexus of subject positions: biracial Asian, growing up in the American West, slightly confused about gender, possibly queer.

Your father's favorite writer is Hemingway, and he continually finds ways to denigrate nonwhite, nonmale, noncishet writers. He constantly refers to Adrienne Rich as Adrienne Bitch, for example, while laughing uproariously at his own joke. When he reads or talks about established BIPOC authors he does so in a way that feels tinged with white saviorism. In magnanimous tones that seem somewhat proprietary, he will pronounce their work as being "really quite good." He doesn't seem to read much contemporary writing, although he's not shy about dismissing it as *crap!* (When, as an adult, you become a published poet, he frequently finds passive aggressive ways to privately convey to you that he thinks your writing, too, is *crap!*)

And so instead of following in your father's footsteps, you obsessively train to be a concert pianist. Asian American girls *do* play the piano after all! Years later, when you write your first poem containing something that resembles Asian American content, you're so confused by what you've done that you have to ask your mentor if it actually even *is* a poem.

It's during one of your hunting trips that your father tells you, for the first time, the story of your parents' marriage. How they met when your father was drafted into the army during the postwar occupation in Japan. How he was assigned to work in the personnel office at Camp Ojima, where your mother had taken a job—apparently as somewhat of a lark, and with the lackadaisical intent of *typing like the sound of rain dropping*. They began a secret courtship, then entered into a secret year-long correspondence when your father returned to the United States. Following that year of separation, your father came back to spend a summer in Japan, during which time they resumed their secret courtship, and your father convinced your mother to run away with him—culminating in their eventual elopement at the end of that summer on August 6, 1955, ten years after the dropping of the atomic bombs. Later on, when you ask your mother why they decided to get married on August 6, she tells you it's because it was the day she *drop the bomb on her family*. You're never quite sure if she's joking about this or not.

4. Japanglish

Your mother speaks Japanese to you when you're an infant and a toddler, and when you first begin to talk, you speak a cryptic form of Japanglish apparently indecipherable to everyone but yourself. Your mother panics. She immediately ceases speaking to you in Japanese. One of her fears has always been that you won't speak proper English. Given your father's profession, she insists that your English-speaking skills will be under close scrutiny. She says she doesn't want to be *blamed* if you turn out to be English *handicapped*. Does it seem to her as if *her* English-speaking skills are under close scrutiny? Does she feel, you wonder, English *handicapped*?

It's a strange thing, not being able to speak your mother's tongue. It's a strange thing having been linguistically disconnected from your mother at the very moment you were learning to speak. It feels a little bit like the way in which your mother switched you from being a left-handed baby to a right-handed baby. She says that she tied down your left hand so that you couldn't use it. She says that she punished you when you reached for things with your left hand. She tells you with pride, in a self-congratulating tone, and likes to remind you that you don't have to use left-handed scissors or sit at left-handed desks at school, thanks to her.

You do know a small handful of words and phrases in Japanese, mostly having to do with food, and when your mother's Japanese friends come to visit, they often forget to switch to English, asking you questions in Japanese, which you're somehow able to answer in

English. Your mother's surprised by this, asking you later how you knew what they were saying. It's not that you can translate verbatim, by any means . . . at best, you only recognize a sprinkling of words here and there. It's difficult for you to explain, but somehow you oftentimes instinctively *know* what the conversations are about.

The limited Japanese you do know falls much more easily, almost naturally, from your tongue than the German or French you were forced to study in high school and college. Is this from consistently having the intonations and rhythms of the Japanese language in your ear? Is it possible people come into the world "hardwired" for a particular language? And if so, what does it mean to have given up a mother tongue one might otherwise have been destined to speak? And if language is in any way a filter through which we perceive and interact with the world, is it possible we turn into completely different people altogether when we speak a different language?

You've carried with you for a number of years a resonant discussion from an online Asian American writer's group about how many members, as children, experienced some type of early "thorniness" with a missing or lost second language. The group went on to speculate that perhaps this was one of the things that informed, at least in part, their need to write. You love this notion of a second "lost" self—a Japanese-speaking self, a "ghostly double" self—that you might be trying to recuperate through your writing. A second self ironically recovered only through an obsessive mastery of the English language. A second self that isn't divided into binaries: American or Japanese. A second self that can speak to her own mother in her mother's native tongue. But still, as much as you might try to write *toward* this second self, you also understand that such an act of recuperation will never actually be possible.

The gaps in translation, the things that don't get said, are funny and awful at the same time. When your first book of poetry comes out in 1999, your mother takes the volume to her ESL class at the University of Wyoming to show her ESL buddies. One of her

Chinese friends reads the first poem in the book, "Pearls." Growing up, you used to love the sound of your mother speaking Japanese on the telephone. You thought it sounded so beautiful, like the sound of birds, maybe sparrows, and you used to think she knew how to speak the language of birds. Inside your head, you had a special name for it. You called it "bird talk." The poem "Pearls" was written in the voice of this child, and early on in the poem, the speaker says her mother "does bird talk" when the Mormons come to the door. When your mother's Chinese ESL friend reads this line, she asks your mother: "Bird talk? Is she mean like pigeon?" Your mother hears, and understands, this question to mean: "Is she mean like pidgin?" As in pidgin (pigeon) English. And no amount of explanation on your part ever since has convinced your mother that this is *not* a poem in which you're accusing her, in a condescending way, of speaking pidgin English.

You would like to learn to speak Japanese. You would like to go to Japan someday. But as an adult, the acquisition of a second language, hardwired or not, is difficult and slow going. In your early thirties, you purchased a Rosetta Stone program for Japanese that was quite good. But even though you practiced assiduously for the better part of a year, you still only learned to say the most trivial and absurd things. *O-hayo gozai-masu.* Good morning. *Sakana wa oyoide masu.* The fish is swimming. Your mother is getting older, and time is running out. How will you ever be able to ask her the important questions? How will you be able to understand her answers? Will she always be asking you things in Japanese, and will you always have to answer back in English—leaving to faith that the part that gets lost in translation will somehow be instinctively *known*?

There's a children's book in which a girl's favorite doll is magically given the ability to speak for one hour, and during that hour, the girl and her doll have to say all the things that went unsaid before and that will otherwise have to go unsaid afterward. You loved that book. You used to think maybe you loved that book so much because you were a girl whose Japanese mother stopped talking to her in Japanese because she wanted her daughter to speak only perfect American English. You sometimes wonder if you could speak Japanese fluently for one hour, what your mother and you would say to each other.

But you understand that this, too, is a kind of fantasy space. One in which, if you only spoke fluent Japanese as a child, your mother would finally understand you. Where she would no longer be cruel. Where she wouldn't ambush you with unexpected borderline rages. Where she wouldn't humiliate you for being such a *stupid-ugly*. Where she wouldn't strike you across the face every time you fidgeted or stimmed or tried to explain a situation she didn't correctly understand. Where she wouldn't threaten to throw you away and give you to the garbage man. Where she wouldn't force you to lie about things that weren't true. Where she wouldn't make up a song to sing just to let you know how dumb you were: *dumb dumb dummy dummy dummy dummy dumb dumb dumb*. Where she wouldn't relentlessly badger you until you were tricked into talking back. Where she wouldn't then wait for your father to get home, needle him into a white-hot fury, until he was goaded into beating you in the basement with paint paddles as punishment for talking back to your mother.

Sometimes you call your mother on the phone and practice your pidgin Japanese. *O-hayo gozai-masu*, you say. *Sakana wa oyoide masu.* She mocks your poor Japanese, answers you in chipped English.

5. Haunted by Landscape

You are haunted by landscape, by the terrifying beauty of mountains, in particular, which you miss with the sort of internal, gaping, physical ache typically reserved for a lost beloved. You think best, and feel the most clarity, in the emotional and intellectual expansiveness of open sky. Is it possible for people to be "imprinted" early on by a particular landscape? And if so, what does it mean to leave, or give up, such a motherland? And if landscape is in any way a filter through which we perceive and interact with the world, is it possible we turn into completely different people altogether when we move to an alternate landscape?

And yet there is an anxiety, too, in this landscape that haunts you. It is a gorgeous and occasionally inhospitable terrain upon which it is difficult to find place/foothold absent the hegemonic tropes of outlaw gunslinger, pioneer, colonizer, entrepreneur. Indeed, it is a terrain upon which you strongly feel it is inappropriate to assert any right to *claim* a nonindigenous place/foothold.

Growing up, you're haunted by the shadows of Heart Mountain, where 10,617 Japanese Americans were imprisoned inside barbed-wire fences and monitored by armed guards during World War II. You're haunted by the racial slurs thrown your way on the elementary school playground. You're haunted by the memory of the doctor's son who lived across the street and molested you when you were nine and who continued to live across the street from you until you finally fled Laramie for college. Years later, you're haunted by the image of Matthew Shepard's broken, pistol-whipped body tied to a fence and left for dead in your hometown. Laramie, the Gem City of the Plains.

You sometimes dream of this landscape, and when you do, it's half nightmare, half rapture. In a prose poem inspired by one of these dreams, you write:

> Coasting down foothills into Laramie. My father's old gray Jeep: vinyled and squared, filigreed in lace cuffs of rust.
>
> Rockies' chilled crust thrusts up hard, distorting the horizon.
>
> Perspective all askew: Mountains much too large and much too blue, looming up much too close too fast. I am not a child, but I slide back and forth in the middle of the front bench seat, knees jogging the gear shift. The parents in the car are not my parents.

Alco's cracked neon on the left closed down years ago. Lost effervescence of wind-bobbled balloons frantically bubbling in the no-longer-there car lot.

Clouds spill down off the mountains, twisting into dangerous, spiraling wraiths.

Are those tornadoes? I ask.

They flame in the too-loud wind like black dry ice, slivered with bright threads of lightning.

Is it war? I ask.

They dervish off the sagebrushed plains toward the road.

You have to stop. You have to pull over, I say. *I'm not wearing a safety belt.*

The sound of unfurling metal, burning, shattered glass, hot wind. Everything goes blank.

An eyelid blinks open to sunlight, emptiness, the heart-shaped white behinds of curious antelope retreating. Empty car, empty highway, everyone else gone. Mountains' bright prong ringing an empty town.

Radio's static crackle, then chipped advertisements, like faded billboards in the wind:

it's Joe Albertson's supermarket . . .

on a sesame seed bun . . .

you're in good hands with All State . . .

And yet you can't seem to let it go. The landscape is too much a part of you, and therefore an indelible part, too, of who you are as a writer. Your relationship to the landscape, though, is not one of inscription, engraving, or carving out and conquering through language. While these settler histories, mythologies, narratives, and texts clearly inhabit, mark, and inform this landscape, your relationship to them, for many reasons, is hostile and vexed. You feel like it is a landscape that deserves so much more than being exploited as a fantasy space upon which to enact and write frontier mythologies. Rather, you wish for it to be a space that *resists* or *talks back to* these familiar settler colonialist tropes. A space where alternate, erased, marginalized, or new and emerging kinds of histories, mythologies, narratives, and texts can emerge and interact.

You're a hybrid in every possible sense of the word—biracial, pansexual, nonbinary, imprinted by East Asian and American Western landscapes and sensibilities—and as such, you can't help but be the sort of writer whose work is complicated and informed by these entangled aspects of identity. You have always been intersectional. You have always been intertextual. A child of the American West, you're always circling through the interconnected margins of Asian American, queer, and gender identities. You're always interrogating, deconstructing, complicating, and unraveling. You will always remain haunted by this liminal fantasy space, this linguistic frontier, this landscape with its hyperbolic vastnesses and dangerously stunning beauty. You cannot let it go.

Sixteen Views of the Bourgeaus

An Homage (Minus Twenty) to Hokusai's Thirty-Six Views of Mount Fuji

1.

Mist fleeces the day's mountains into the mostly hypothetical. Ravens, all sudden glossand caw, slice through like sleek black jets.

2.

June, and you're spending the month at the Banff Centre in Alberta, Canada, for a self-directed writing residency. You're here in part because as an aspiring concert pianist during your teens, one of your fantasies was to take summer master classes in Banff. Exploring the grounds for the first time when you arrive, you soon discover the cluster of music huts below the sharply angled shadow of Mount Rundle—an image you recognize with an uncanny pang. You suddenly remember a brochure whose alluringly glossy pages you often daydreamed over—pages filled with musicians, artists, grand jeté-ing ballet dancers, and swoon-inducing pictures of the Canadian Rockies. Where did that brochure come from? Did your piano teacher give it to you? Or did you send off for it yourself?

Who was that girl who wanted nothing more than to practice piano all day long in one of those huts? You used to get up at 4:00

a.m. every morning to practice for three hours before school. On weekends and summers, you practiced eight hours a day. You sometimes think that you were trying to practice yourself *elsewhere*—somewhere, anywhere out of Wyoming. Standing outside the Banff music huts over three decades later feels like bumping into your young self during a time travel glitch, thereby risking a potential violation of Star Fleet's Temporal Prime Directive. Sometimes, as you're writing in the studio with your window open, faint curlicues of music wisp up to your room in fragrant spirals of sound.

3.

Day after day, you stare at the mountains, visually tractor beamed onto them like some cyberstalking lovestruck creeper on Facebook—obsessively studying the beloved's different facial expressions by combing through their profile pics, helplessly clicking *Like, Like, Like* . . .

4.

After each meal, you take a picture with your iPhone—each time, the same picture from the same spot—to track the mountain range's rapidly shifting moods and costumes. You've been posting these images as visual updates to Facebook. You've also been thinking about Hokusai's famous wood-block series, *Thirty-Six Views of Mount Fuji*. Are your iPhone snaps a playful, postmodern homage to Hokusai? Thirty-Six Views in the age of mechanical reproduction? All of this makes you wonder, though, if there's something too easy/too instant about our point-and-click lives. Have we rendered completely irrelevant the artistry, for example, of Hokusai's meticulously graven images? In our glib and now-rote insistence on the failure of representation, has our cultural moment become all self-conscious *artlessness* and no art? And is our tendency toward fast-food representation (instantly made, shared, consumed) a spineless mimesis or a rigorously mirrored critique? Still, even if it's a little Borg-y, there's an attentiveness to the moment, an electric spontaneity, a communal sense of call and response in the networked sharing of thought and image. The spider plucks the interwebs as if to say: *Look at this! Look at this!* Linked-in responders call back: *I see! I see!* Even Hokusai, with the wood-block print, was ultimately creating a mechanical reproduction for mass sharing.

5.

A cloud curls up like a plump white cat on the sharply slanted slope of Mount Rundle early in the afternoon and naps there until suppertime.

6.

The first day out after days of rain and writing, you clamber down Tunnel Mountain into the town of Banff. You walk by the Bow River, visit Central Park, circle around downtown a few times, and take pictures from the Bow River Bridge. Late in the afternoon, you spontaneously decide to explore the Bow Falls Trail. Manic from sunlight, giddily overstimulated, and stupidly dehydrated, you find yourself completely turned around and alone in the woods on one of the lesser, unpaved hiking paths. Naturally, you begin to obsess madly about bears. Saner parts of your brain realize you're still close enough to town for bears to be more of an anomaly than not, and you're sure that other hikers and tourists are nearby, even if you can't see them. You fret about having chewing gum on your person. You take your bear bell out and clip it to the lanyard on your backpack, but its ineffectual jingling just makes you feel silly. Saner parts of your brain realize your fretting isn't even really about *bears*, per se, but about not having your bear*ings*. About feeling lonely, unknown, unmoored. Like an astronaut floating in the heart-stopping beauty of outer space on the end of a single slim umbilical.

7.

Just below Bow Falls, there's a rush of cool air flecked with effervescent bits of the Bow River churned and frothed into a refreshing spritz. The falls widen out into a large pool, which then forks northward into the Bow River, and southbound into the Spray River. At this point of widening, snow-capped and snow-striped peaks rise up out of the water into a Wedgewood-blue sky like hallucinatory meringue. Confectionary clouds puff above like nozzled wads of whipped cream, caramelizing the snowy peaks below with burnt-sugar shadows. It's an overwhelming confluence of almost-too-pretty-to-be-true things in stylized concert with one another—a sort of surrealistically over-the-top Rococo minuet.

8.

In the dining room, backdropped by a dark armada of fast-moving clouds, Japanese twin toddlers deploy their bananas as telephones. One pokes out eyeholes in his slice of cheddar, then regards you from behind his mask of cheese.

9.

Seven days in, and you wake up in the middle of the night, heart pounding, convinced you're doing your writing residency entirely wrong, that you're wasting time and opportunities, and that all the poems you've written so far are completely hopeless. In fact, the entire project from which you're attempting to generate these hopeless poems is, you realize with the epiphanic lucidity of 4:00 a.m., completely hopeless as well, and your hopeless-project-generating brain is (why did you not see this *before*?) the mothership of complete hopelessness. By now, you're crackly skinned and feverish, nose-diving your way toward a full-fledged panic attack—smoke spiraling out of your engine, gas tank ready to explode into flame. You desperately forage for Ativan in your one-quart TSA-approved Ziploc baggie, only to discover there's only one left. You debate saving it for "just in case." Just in case of what, you're not exactly sure. Maybe psychological Armageddon? You go ahead and take it, which initiates a shitstorm of anxiety about future and worser incidents of middle-of-the-night meltdowns. Waiting for the Ativan to kick in, you open your window to let in the cool mountain air. Where are the deer who like to nibble on dandelions outside your window? Where do they go at night?

10.

In heavy mist, the scent of pine turns brighter. The train whistle's a smooth round pebble radio-waving infinitely outward in its pooled milk of mist. Locomotive wheels rattle the track: *Clacketty clack. Clacketty clack.*

11.

Dinner, and the mountain range is obscured into nonexistence by rain and mist. The horizon seems curtained by heavy shantung silver silk. There's a swirled nebula of grey in the bottom left corner, backlit by a half-hearted pock of sunlight. Before long, though, the mist begins to dissolve, like cotton candy on the tongue. Bit by bit, the curtain fronting the mountains goes from opaque, to semisheer, to sheer. It's like watching a Polaroid develop while eating a bowl of Madras rutabaga soup. The Polaroid's a metaphor. The soup isn't. The soup's so delicious it makes the entire surface of your tongue squirm with pleasure. It makes your lips tingle. It's so delicious you eat it *accelerando*—each consecutive spoonful coming faster and faster on the heels of the last. By the time you reach the bottom of the bowl, the mountains have broken through the last gauzy bits of misted veil and you have achieved a certain level of clarity.

12.

Pilot Mountain's peak grazes and pierces the soft dark underbellies of low-flying clouds. Even though it's sunny everywhere else, blue-gray rays of rain downspout onto the mountain range like streams of water squirting from pinpricked water balloons.

13.

You're eavesdropping during lunch. A young woman tells a table full of Canadians about her road trip through the United States. "I drove for, like, forty hours," she says, "and it was all flat. Not like here." She gestures out the window at the Bourgeaus, which obligingly thrust up out of the horizon in bright blue clarity—pepperminty stripes of snow glittering in the sun. A few minutes later she notes, "I didn't like South Dakota. It was too kitschy and touristy. But the Badlands," she adds as an afterthought, "were nice."

14.

On the Sulphur Mountain gondola, you ride with two Chinese women, a mother and a daughter. Their red plastic name tags indicate they're on a Charming Holiday. You're being strung up the side of a very tall mountain—like a clear glass bead on a metal wire—in an ovum-shaped capsule that holds four. The daughter, middle-aged, keeps changing seats in the gondola, making it lurch until it starts to feel less like a glass bead and more like a trembling raindrop wobbling on a wire. Finally settled in, she eyeballs you rigorously, confers with her mother in Cantonese. "Chinese?" the daughter asks you. "Japanese," says the mother. "Half Japanese," you say. They discuss this animatedly among themselves, occasionally gesturing in your direction. The mother reaches over and pats your arm. She pulls out her gondola ticket and points to it. "How much you pay?" Extremely pleased by your answer, they laugh happily as you slide by Mount Brewster, which seems to be trying on a whimsical hat made out of clouds for size.

15.

Alternating ravens smoothly yo-yo up and down wind's taut flicked strings.

16.

At the Sanson Peak Meteorological Station on top of Sulphur Mountain, a golden-mantled ground squirrel poses for pictures, then sits and gazes pensively toward the Bourgeaus from a rocky outcropping. The afternoon cycles rapidly between rain, sleet, mist, and hot blasts of sunlight. With each change in weather, the mountains are completely reinvented. The Bow Valley vista is so beautiful it makes your heart hurt. But it's really those shape-shifters, the clouds, who haunt you. There's no place you'd rather be than high in the mountains, brushing up against the clouds. At the same time, you always have an uncanny sense of trespass—a sense of having intruded someplace not necessarily meant for you, or maybe even for human beings in general.

You feel uneasily enthralled by clouds. Ethereal yet dangerous, they distort and disrupt space, time, perception. There's something otherworldly in their shape-shifting fluidity, their transformative powers, the ontological ease with which they move between being and nothingness.

And so you take a cue from the golden-mantled ground squirrel. You stop taking pictures, put away your camera, and find a quiet place to sit by yourself. You think of the unlikelihood of being here. You think about the unlikelihood of anyone being *anywhere*. You think about being and not being. You think about nothingness. You think about being and not thinking. You stop thinking and try to simply be—slowly opening yourself into pure aperture in this numinous house of clouds, this blue-domed spirit jar, this lonely summit of misty hosannas.

Ghost-Busting in Wickenburg

A Resurrection of Sorts

In the photograph, you stand with your American grandmother in a trailer park retirement community in Wickenburg, Arizona. She wears a taupe windbreaker—a nylon scarf covering her hair and tied beneath her chin. Are her eyes disguised behind sunglasses? You have on a brown houndstooth dress with a Peter Pan collar, a honey-colored neckerchief, cable-knit stockings, and patent leather shoes. Your hair's been Dippity Do'd into the residual shape of a pink plastic curler sausaging either side of your head. Your grandmother holds your hand. You are four years old.

Who's taking the picture? Your father? Your American grandfather? You can't remember.

It's your first time visiting your American grandparents in Arizona, where they have come to retire. It's your first time riding on a plane, which is an elegant and luxurious affair. Your parents dress up: your father in a trench coat and hat, your mother in stockings and heels. During the flight, dinner is served with cloth napkins, real china, and wine. The flight attendants give you a small waxy packet of crayons and a coloring book. They sashay up and down the aisles in saucy hats, go-go boots, and bright-buttoned uniforms. They bring around baskets sparkling with mounds of wrapped candy.

On the way through Denver there's a long layover at the airport, so you take a taxicab to the zoo. You've never been in a cab before, much less a zoo, and you're particularly shocked by the hippopotamuses in their too-small pools clotted with huge green mounds of poo. The smell is terrible, but you can't stop staring. Back at the Denver Airport, which is dotted with souvenir shops glittering with exotically themed kitsch, you ride up and down the escalator. You are heady with urbanity and cosmopolitanism. Suddenly, you're on your way somewhere, *anywhere*, and this giddy precipice of departure is the start of a love/hate affair with restlessness.

◎

May 2012, and you're visiting your friend Natalie in Arizona. You're trying to find the trailer in Wickenburg where you visited your grandparents as a child. It's been decades. Your memories consist of sharp brief sparks of sensory impressions: white aluminum siding accented with strips of pink paneling. A small door with steps in between the kitchen and living room that came down to an asphalt patio where you first learned to roller skate. A DIY aluminum shed your grandfather built near the front rear of the trailer. An aluminum carport on the other side where your grandfather parked his truck. One year, your grandfather and you planted seeds from an orange you ate, and you remember being thrilled by the little sprig of green that spiked up by the back steps a week later.

◎

Between the ages of four and nine, you visited Wickenburg with your parents every other year, at Christmas. When you think of Christmas now, you always think of palm trees, cacti, the quiet glow of homemade luminaria limning rock-gardened pathways. You can still remember many of the Christmas presents you received during visits to Arizona with a peculiar pang of loss and pleasure:

A dictionary-sized Peanuts book with a pull string—mostly all hollow box with a thin layer of glossy pages on top. The pull string attached to a plastic ring on the side. A miracle of technology! When you pulled the string, the characters' voices narrated the story. You remember how, when you opened this present, you suddenly become self-conscious, unsure of how you were supposed to act, so you performatively exclaimed—mimicking the exact tones of one of the Christmas commercials you'd seen on TV—"It's the ideal holiday gift!" The adults all laughed at you, and you felt both pleased and anxious.

A Minnie Mouse Timex with a yellow wristband. A real watch that told real time! A watch you're only allowed to wear for special occasions. You take it in and out of its box, holding it to your ear to listen to its famed takes-a-licking ticking until your mother takes it away from you and hides it somewhere for safekeeping.

Another year there's a Hippity Hop—a big rubber ball to bounce on with a handle on the middle. The sound of red rubber smacking against the asphalt patio of your grandparents' trailer home creates a satisfying reverberation, like the slightly metallic ricochet of a giant basketball.

Or a game of Tiddlywinks, with brightly colored plastic disks called "winks" and the larger disks, called "squidgers," used to propel the winks into a cup. And jacks, which your mother always beat you at. Checkers, too, and roller skates.

Maybe the best present of all, though, is a turquoise dog, made for you by a friend of your grandparents who you call Uncle Arthur. Large, rough-hewn, chunky, but definitively *dog*-shaped, it hangs on the end of a multicolored hand-beaded necklace. You wear it everywhere you go, and when you feel worried, you rub the turquoise dog for luck.

◎

After visiting a thrift store, a coffee shop/ice cream parlor, and the Wickenburg Public Library, you and Natalie idly drive through several retirement communities. One is almost close enough for you to say, yes, it was *like* this. There's a trailer that's *sort of*, but *not quite*, the trailer you're looking for: white and pinkish, but with a sliding glass door and a more elaborate sun port. Close enough for you to say, yes, it was *like* this. The almost-but-not-quite-ness, though, has whetted your appetite. You feel as if you're hot on the trail of your own ghost—the awkward and anxious child you used to be, and maybe still are in many respects, who you've spent your life trying to erase or disguise. And so the search begins in earnest. You phone your parents for more information. They tell you the name of the retirement community, although there isn't an exact number for the trailer. iPhones are deployed, an address is Googled, and GPS technology blue-dots a route to the Dessert Cypress Retirement Community.

◎

When your American grandparents met, your grandmother was teaching at the Clark Street School in the copper mining town of Jerome, Arizona. Your grandfather had recently returned from serving in France during World War I—he'd joined up underage, requiring a reluctantly extracted note of permission from his mother. Back in the States, your grandfather enrolled in UC Berkeley to study petroleum engineering, earning his college tuition by working the Jerome copper mines during the summer.

Once known as the wildest town in the West, Jerome is now a charmingly eccentric artists' community precariously perched atop Cleopatra Hill. It's marketed to tourists as the "Largest Ghost Town in America." Today, Jerome (population approximately five hundred) is filled with quirky houses and shops, historic buildings, and breathtaking vistas. The Clark Street School, which has undergone several incarnations—including a particularly weird stint during the 1970s as a disco—now serves as the Jerome Town Hall, and several of the old classrooms have been restored in time for the annual Jerome Home Tour. How marvelously strange it is to wander through the same hallways and rooms where your enterprising and young American grandmother worked as a schoolteacher during the 1920s.

According to your grandmother, she was walking by the train station after work one day with her girlfriend—also a teacher at the Clark Street School—when they saw two young men getting off the train. Your grandmother's girlfriend looked them over carefully, before pointing to one and saying, "That one's mine. You can have the other one." The "other one" was your grandfather. Your grandmother was apparently fine with this divvying up of boys, though, because the "other one" was the one she'd wanted all along.

After they were married, your grandmother moved into the little miner's shack that your grandfather was renting for the summer, down toward the base of Cleopatra Hill, and they honeymooned there. Many years later, after selling their ranch in Lander, Wyoming, your grandparents decided to move back to Arizona, near the place where they'd first met and married.

You wish you'd had more time to get to know your American grandmother. You suppose she was a product of her era in many ways—a proper young lady brought up in Pasadena, California, the City of Roses. Yet, in so many other ways, she was undeniably *modern*. She earned a college degree, then went on to help put her younger sisters through college by working as a telephone switchboard operator. She loved to write. What on earth was she thinking when she decided to come and teach in the rough-and-tumble mining town of Jerome, Arizona—a boomtown filled with nefarious characters and an infamous row of brothels? (Her pedagogical technique apparently included immediately befriending the largest and roughest-looking boy in the class as an ally, to help maintain order.) You can only conclude that she was independent, strong-willed, adventurous. Later, when she embraced your grandfather's lifelong dream of owning a ranch in Wyoming, she worked there as an equal partner—raising sheep and cattle. She learned how to ride horses, shoot rattlesnakes, and rescue orphaned lambs. Apparently, your grandmother was a woman who sometimes liked to have it both ways. Apparently, your grandmother was a woman who wanted what she wanted. Sometimes, your Japanese mother likes to say in acidic tones that the person you resemble most is your American grandmother.

◎

When you first spot your grandparents' old trailer, after Natalie patiently circles through the Dessert Cypress Retirement Community several times, there's still some uncertainty—a crossing off of a mental checklist against fractured bits of memory. You get out of the car and peer into the window of the front door, and that's when you know it's the one you've been looking for. Memory, Google, logic, and instinct all suddenly intersect like a final puzzle piece clicking into place. You're startled by the intense physicality of *knowing* you've been here before. You feel as if time has doubled back in on itself and you've met yourself both coming and going.

Peering into the shadowy interior of the empty trailer, you see everything again with a strange clarity. The Naugahyde recliner where your grandfather sometimes let you curl up with him. The knitting basket by your grandmother's chair, where she sometimes liked to brush your hair. The sofa where you slept at night and read picture books checked out from the Wickenburg Public Library. The blue-flame smell of the gas stove and the hot scratch of the match when your grandfather made oatmeal for you in the mornings. The shock of finding a set of false teeth bubbling in a glass jar of Pepsodent in the bathroom. The soft sputter of shuffled cards, velvety with use, when your grandmother taught you how to play solitaire.

You remember that during your first visit, in the guest bedroom where your parents slept, there was foam padding sticking out from in between the mattress and the bed frame. It was yellowed, dry, and brittle with age, and when you touched it, a piece of it broke off into your hand. You remember how your father, who'd just returned from hunting with your grandfather in the desert, found you with the broken piece of foam in your hand and immediately blew his stack in one of his sudden and volatile rages. How he was screaming at you as he dragged you out into the living room, where he gave you a brutal spanking in front of your mother and your grandparents. You were humiliated, of course, because you wanted your grandparents to *like* you, and now everything seemed ruined. How your father offered you up to your grandfather, asked if he would like to give you "a walloping" as well. You remember how your grandfather, as if to defuse the situation, quietly pulled out the dead quail from his canvas hunting pouch and showed them to you instead. The metallic smell of their feathers matted in blood. Their slack downy necks. How you gently stroked their soft heads with your index finger. The iridescent curl of their plumes.

You remember your grandfather's reloading machine in the aluminum shed. Fascinating machinery of levers and weights. Peppery smell of gun powder, the pie-crimped plastic of yellow shells, the bright rattle of birdshot pellet. The same pellets that pinged onto the plates at dinner time when you ate the tiny-boned quail your mother pan fried in salt, pepper, and flour.

You remember the beautiful shapes of saguaro, prickly pear, and beavertail cactus. The agave, the aloe vera, and the rattling yucca pods you liked to collect. How the primly pompous rows of walking quail contrasted so funnily with the Pigpen-like flurried joy of their dust baths. You remember the roadrunners with cleverly tilting heads and tails that loped so sleekly through the trailer court.

You step away from the door of the empty trailer and study the For Sale sign in front. You want to buy it. You don't think it should belong to anyone else. And that's when you recognize the landscaped island of beavertail cactus where the picture was taken with your grandmother.

And you finally remember your grandmother's blue eyes behind the dark glasses. Her quiet, insistent voice. Your hand held there for just a moment again inside the soft dry crease of hers.

Derby Dreams

1. Kansas City Bomber

Kansas City Bomber is completely to blame. Raquel Welch, in the role of roller derby queen K.C. Carr—all honey-colored hair and velocity, all shiny nylon, and striped tube socks—fiercely caroms around the tilted edges of a banked roller derby track. She jabs and bumps and collides and brawls—matter-of-factly jumping over the fallen bodies of derby girls downed on the track. She illicitly charges off the bench and clobbers "Horrible Hank" Hopkins with a mop. She fights dirty. During "The Star Spangled Banner," she snaps her gum and rakishly winks at two of her lovestruck female fans. That's how we know she's one tough cookie.

It's 1972, the second Golden Age of derby. The relatively nascent National Organization for Women is campaigning to secure passage of the Equal Rights Amendment (ERA), which bars discrimination on the basis of sex. The National Women's Political Caucus is formed the year before, and in 1973, the Supreme Court will affirm a woman's right to privacy in *Roe v. Wade*. Popular movies in 1972 include *The Godfather, Deepthroat*, and *Last Tango in Paris*. Watergate unfolds. Atari releases PONG. *Cosmopolitan*, *Ladies Home Journal*, and *Ms. Magazine* simultaneously show up in your parents' house, on loan from the Albany County Public Library in Laramie,

Wyoming, with apparently little or no cognitive dissonance whatsoever. It's 1972, and Adrienne Rich opens her poem "Planetarium" with the shape-shiftingly transgressive image of "a woman in the shape of a monster / a monster in the shape of a woman / the skies are full of them." Later on in this poem, written for unacknowledged astronomer Caroline Herschel, Rich writes: "I have been standing all my life in the / direct path of a battery of signals / the most accurately transmitted most / untranslatable language in the universe."

As a biracial Nisei daughter, you know, even from a very early age, the things you're *supposed* to want for yourself. You take ballet and piano lessons. You're supposed to get a Ph.D. You should want to become a medical doctor. Femininity is obligatory, but you're also not supposed to be too silly or girly or frilly if you want to be taken seriously. Your secret aspirations for yourself are darker, closeted, and much more incoherent however. You want to drive a fire truck. Or become a stripper.

Your parents police every single aspect of how you're allowed to be in your own body. Anything less than mindless compliance is a punishable offense. Yet when you're nine years old, and you're molested by the eighteen-year-old boy who lives across the street, your parents blame you for not putting up more of a fight. At school, you're relentlessly bullied for being shy, awkward, bookish, and biracial. Even though you're just a child, your body feels like a contested site, and you find yourself butting up against expectations and obligations that seem to come attached de facto to race and gender. You wish for bodily autonomy. You aspire to serious badassery. And so the night you finally see *Kansas City Bomber* on your parents' black-and-white TV, three or four years after its theater release, you find that it magically articulates an unnamed desire—a desire that hybridizes the battery of conflicting cultural signals, the bifurcated impulses of fireman and stripper, into something tangible and coherent: a dream of becoming a roller derby queen.

That Christmas you lobby hard for roller skates, and although the ones you get are, disappointingly, the strap-on kind that buckle over your tennis shoes, you skate around and around and around your parents' unfinished basement, viciously hip checking your imaginary opponents.

2. A Brief and Much-Needed Letter to Your Fourth Grade Self

Dear Fourth Grade Self:

Since this is about the time when you begin to feel particularly fucked in the head about body image, and race, and orientation, and gender, I want you to know that eventually there will be an all-Asian derby team called Rice, who will bout with an all-Mexican derby team called Beans. Eventually there will be Asian derby queens, with names like Kamikaze Kim and Rice Rocket. Your secret derby name for your inner derby girl will be Bruise Lee.

Back to the Future-ishly Yours,

Me

3. Rink Rash

> Re-vision—the act of looking back, of seeing with fresh eyes, of entering an old text from a new critical direction—is for woman more than a chapter in cultural history: it is an act of survival. Until we understand the assumptions in which we are drenched we cannot know ourselves. And this drive to self-knowledge, for women, is more than a search for identity: it is part of our refusal of the self-destructiveness of male-dominated society.
>
> —ADRIENNE RICH, "When We Dead Awaken: Writing as Re-Vision"

Years later, when you watch *Kansas City Bomber* again, you're surprised at the things you've either misremembered, or blocked, from your memory of the film. For example, you remembered K.C. Carr as a sexy badass—one who makes good by the end of the movie as a result of her skating and brawling superpowers. But as it turns out, K.C. isn't even a derby queen entirely by choice—rather, she's forced into it through the desperate circumstances of being a divorced mother under economic duress. You forgot that K.C. had children (including a tough-talking roller-skating urchin of a daughter played by a young Jodie Foster). You completely blocked many of the scenes that took place off the track, in which K.C.'s drably garbed in cardigans, pleated skirts, pantyhose, and pumps—looking not so much like a roller derby queen but more like a steno from the typing pool. When K.C. visits her home in Fresno, her strident mother—who takes care of K.C.'s children while she's on the derby circuit—nags and shames and emotionally bullies K.C., while K.C.'s son rejects her timid overtures to bond with him and runs away from her.

As it turns out, the movie is, in many respects, an unsettling exploration of the vulnerability of commodified and commodifiable bodies. The skaters work under constant threat of serious injury, worrying about how their aging bodies will hold up against younger players. As in the world of professional wrestling, when these bodies are used up, they're discarded. Aging alcoholic derby diva Jackie Burdett is terrified of being dethroned by K.C., which causes her to sink to increasingly belligerent depths of alcohol-fueled depression. Similarly, "Horrible Hank" Hopkins, also aging, and possibly concussion addled as well, frets about ways to increase his worth to the team—scheming up performative spectacles in which he antagonizes the crowd by making pig noises.

Female bodies are rendered doubly vulnerable—their participation in a gender-transgressive spectacle seemingly codes them as sexually available objects. Following a bout, for example, K.C. and a teammate fight off would-be rapists (male derby fans who first solicit autographs from them) outside the derby venue. Likewise, when K.C. is summarily traded from the Kansas City Bombers to the Portland Loggers after losing a grudge match to Big Bertha Baglioni, she's revealed to be a mere pawn in the hands of repugnantly smug derby impresario and league owner Burt Henry. Immediately following her move to Portland, Burt plies K.C. with a nice dinner and the impressive view from his fancy bachelor pad, after which K.C. compliantly becomes his lover. In classically abusive fashion, he systematically isolates K.C. from her friends and support system—trading her roommate, Lovey, to a team in Denver, and firing her friend "Horrible Hank." Burt promises to make K.C. a roller derby star on TV, but tells her she won't be able to bring her children along. "I'm so lonely," K.C. sighs, and Burt tells her that he loves her, inasmuch as he's capable of loving anyone.

And so it seems the K.C. Carr you selectively remember from the movie is in many ways a wishful construction on your part—possibly the K.C. Carr that you wanted or needed her to be.

4. Derby Girls of the Corn

Bemidji Babe City Rollers
Bizman Bombshells
Fargo Moorhead Furies
Grand Forx Sugarbeaters
Iron Range Maidens
Moose Lake Mafia
Nodak Knockouts
Norfolk Bruizin' Bettys
Oskaloosa Mayhem
Sioux Falls Killa Beez

5. Derby Gurlesque

Jump-cut to the Long Lines Family Rec Center in Sioux City, Iowa, where the Sioux City Roller Dames have a bout with the Sioux Falls Roller Dollz. Derby, which originated in the Midwest, has gone through several revivals, and the most recent flat-track renaissance has come home to roost once again in flyover country. Throughout the Great Plains, roller dolls (and dames and broads and vixens) with sassy derby names and muscular thighs, glittered and brightly tattooed, are migrating every weekend like glorious birds on buses from bout to bout, rec center to rec center, across rivers and fields and corn.

In shorts and skirts, in zombie and pirate makeup, in fishnet and spandex, these dames and dolls have gone third wave. Their strapping rough-and-tumble toughness brazenly deconstructs retrograde notions of gender. At the same time, their over-the-top costuming simultaneously reappropriates and embraces the grrly, the femme, while underscoring its performativity, its constructedness. They're serious athletes in drag. They bring to bear the aesthetic influences of punk rock, rockabilly, and burlesque. They're body positive and sex positive. They're both butch and femme. They are fluid, transgressive, genderqueer.

Postmodern derby girls destabilize and resist easy commodification through proffering burlesqued performances of their derby alter egos—personas that offer the audience a series of slippery signifiers that mock as much as they titillate. Using these constructed characters, they reappropriate, take control of, and author the terms of their commodification for their own pleasure and benefit. This is particularly evident in the derby names they give to themselves. This power to name, and the ways in which the rollergirls name themselves—names that revel in sexual and linguistic play, that gleefully dismantle conventions of gender, femininity, sexuality, and power—similarly tantalize and mock: Queen Elizabitch, Shimmy Hoffa, Yoko Oh No You Didn't, Felony Convixen, Betsy Wrecksie, Morgan LeFaetal.

Unlike the banked-track derby of the 1970s represented in *Kansas City Bomber*, twenty-first-century derby's spectacle resides not in out-and-out choreographed brawling on the track (reminiscent, in many respects, of the moves and antics of professional wrestling) but rather in burlesque flair combined with a more serious attentiveness to the actual sport of the bout itself. In fact, at the pinnacle of the sport, the teams that compete in the finals of the Women's Flat Track Derby Association are made up of professional, world-class athletes. Derby girls train long and hard. It's a sport that requires endurance, strength, mad skating skillz, and strategy. WFTDA penalties are strict for fighting, tripping, elbow jabbing, back blocking, and head blocking, and team members are required to wear helmets, pads, and guards. Still, there are bone-crunching falls, and massive pileups. The skaters are fast and fierce and fearless. Your favorite Sioux Falls Roller Dollz include rangy jammers Jackie O'Smashus and Julia Wild, as well as the quick vicious pixies, Funsize and Applicious. You are also partial to the rosy-cheeked, milkmaid-esque blockers Red Thunder and The Annihilatrix.

Maybe they are like your wishful, misremembered construction of K.C. Carr. They are the embodiment of who you wished to be as an awkward and troubled girl, skating around and around by herself in her parents' basement in Laramie, Wyoming, and you love them for it.

6. Afterimage: Heartbeat of the Pulsar

In the derby photographs you take, the star-helmeted jammers, in the rec center's glaring yellow neon, are hot circling streaks of whiz and blur—*every impulse of light exploding / from the core / as life flies out of us*—like pictures of Ferris wheels spiraling in the night.

Loop-de-loop

1. Badlands Loop

South Dakota, 240 Badlands Loop Road in May, and the ornate burbled warbling of meadowlarks echoes in melodic veronicas throughout the spires, buttes, pinnacles, and gullies of sedimentary stone. The Badlands have donned a frilly spring dress in bright sour-apple greens, saffron yellows, and dusted-silk pinks. The scent of sage and sweetgrass smudges the still-cool air.

You've just completed a grueling semester—complicated by having to avoid your sexual harasser, a departmental colleague, while the sexual harassment complaint played out. Your parents have "disowned" you, yet again—this time over a poem that their across-the-street neighbors printed off from the internet for them, thinking they'd be pleased. You haven't been able to write. And so you're running away from home—exchanging a fretful mound of worry for yellow mounds and prairie dog pups.

For three days, you circle the loop, stopping at whim for pictures and hikes, until the rhythms of the loop's contours and hairpin curves take on the delirious and swoon-stunned familiarity of a new lover's body: your favorite leftover dollop of red-ribboned Brule islanded like an afterthought in the green center of White River Valley; the turnoff for Sage Creek Rim Road, where you go to look for burrowing owls amid the noisy coteries of prairie dogs; the collapsed Bundt-cake folds of the Bigfoot Overlook.

Late May's clouds circle above either like wobbly, nozzled wads of coffee-shop foam or sleek, dark-bellied leviathans. Wild goats make a loop through the grasslands where they graze all day, before emerging at sunset to sun themselves on the sandstone cliffs, bringing evening's cars to a gawking halt near the Pinnacles entrance. Underneath its upside-down commas of horns, one of the goats peers down at you from a ledge and blinks into the flickering shutter of your camera lens, his eyes iconic and slow as gold cat's eye marbles.

2. Swoop

Unexpected wingbeat, talon, and spray of gold flint sparking the light when one of the golden eagles surfing currents near the Sharps Formation by Castle Trail suddenly plummets to dip and whorl just yards in front of your Jeep. It seems curious. Its sharp-eyed gaze sees you staring at it through the windshield, and in that moment, you are no longer the voyeur with a camera, but the spied upon. The eagle loops around for another flyby before swirling skyward again, and for those brief moments, you are all spotlight halo and golden blaze.

3. Toxic Tape Loop

Like the prehistoric flyways of a migratory bird of misery, you have your very own Badlands Loop in your brain. This migratory bird of misery looks something, you think, like a Pteranodon. Genus name: *Stupid*, species name: *ugly*. The *Stupid ugly* bird, more commonly known as *Unlovable*. The migration loop of *Unlovable* is so deeply ingrained and imprinted it's created great stuck ruts—scars or wounds—in the neural pathways of the sky. Unsurprisingly,

Unlovable has a prehistoric, walnut-sized brain, whose hypervigilant limbic system goes straight to DEFCON 1 at the first threat of danger, launching *Unlovable* skyward into its mournful parabolas. *Unlovable* comes with a self-destruct button and isn't afraid to use it. Of course, everyone knows how things worked out for the dinosaurs, so *Unlovable* has had to learn how to get themself unstuck from these ruts. And even if they risk getting lost by taking an unfamiliar loop, at least now there's Siri to help them find their way.

4. Spirograph

One of your most longingly coveted and favorite childhood toys was Hasbro's Spirograph. The fabulous emergence of the repetitive looped patterns was hypnotic, and you spent hours rotating the brightly colored pens within and around the plastic mechanical gears. The dizzyingly filigreed spirals seemed, somehow, elaborately constructed yet absolutely organic. Unexpectedly random yet pleasingly symmetrical. Created by mathematical roulette curves, this feeling of simultaneous chance and order made an emerging sense out of chaos. You remember how drawing the spiraling patterns felt like playing music, how the delicately elaborate hypotrochoids and epitrochoids seemed to visually represent the intricate precision of Baroque keyboard music. They *looked* like what it *felt* like to play a Bach Invention, Toccata, or Fugue.

5. Perception Feedback Loop

Shadow hollowed and wind ruffled, the contours of the Badlands—sometimes like stiff-beaten cake batter, sometimes like striated molten glass—shape-shift beneath cloud dapple and light with the chameleon mimetic grace of the X-men's Mystique: here, a sad woman weeps into long spidery fingers; here, a tired elephant rests its trunk on the ground to feel for seismic disturbances; here, cubist lovers share a stilled stone kiss for eternity. This mercurial fluidity, this sense of vast movement and flow having been suddenly flash frozen is an illusion, of course, a brisk flicker of movement spied out of the corner of one's eye. Or is the rock's geologic perdurability the true illusion, based on our own microscopic perceptions of time? If one were to speed up the tape, collapsing millennia into milliseconds, wouldn't it reveal the dynamic geological flux of deposition and erosion? The crazed, apocalyptic scatter of ammonites and clams in the wake of an ocean spilling out of its mountain-cracked basin? In only a mere blink of geological time, the Badlands will disappear entirely.

6. Plague and Peanut Butter

Embroidering the grasslands like a series of loose running stitches, the intricately networked prairie dog tunnels of the Conata Basin serves as one of the largest and most important recovery sites for the near-extinct black-footed ferret. Black-footed ferrets became extinct in the wild in the late 1980s but are being bred in captivity and released—microchipped, radio telemetried, and vaccinated—into prairie dog colonies such as the Conata Basin. Prairie dogs provide the main food source for black-footed ferrets, and the prairie dog burrows also provide shelter. But the prairie dogs, too, are in danger of decimation by sylvatic plague, which is spread by fleas. Fish and wildlife scientists have been attempting to control the spread of plague through individually dusting prairie dog burrows for fleas—a process that's proven unsustainable in terms of cost in labor and time. Now they've been working on an oral vaccine that can be disseminated in the field through baits. Although initially not so interested in plain baits, the prairie dogs have apparently demonstrated a strong predilection for peanut butter flavored baits. So will this be how the black-footed ferrets are ultimately saved and a plague held at bay? By a ubiquitous love for peanut butter?

7. Chinatown of the Mind

In Deadwood, South Dakota, five dollars buys a golden ticket down the stairs of the Gold Nugget Trading Post into a labyrinth of underground tunnels alleged to be the remnants of Deadwood's Chinatown. Mostly a tourist trap, and heavy on kitsch, the China Tunnel Tour capitalizes on scintillating notions of opium dens and highlights include a giant red dragon, as well as a Loony Toons–esque seven-foot Buddha carved out of rose quartz (the state mineral of South Dakota)—essentialized ideas of a Chinatown standing in as symbolic shorthand for the more complex histories of Deadwood's Chinese settlers. Archaeological evidence, for example, indicates that the China Tunnel Tour's tunnels don't even fall within the actual limits of Deadwood's historic Chinatown. Located on the northern side of Main Street in Deadwood Gulch, between Deadwood proper and Elizabethtown, Chinatown was situated in what was sometimes referred to as the Badlands, where operations of vice—brothels, gambling, saloons, and opium dens—were also located. The Badlands would have been where the small pox "pest tent" from HBO's *Deadwood* was quarantined. Calamity Jane was also said to have lived in Deadwood's Badlands.

In retrospect, the extreme hardships of the Chinese immigration to the American West during this time period—a difficult sea crossing, grueling and dangerous labor, violence, and racism—seems almost as unlikely as space travel. Deadwood itself was an illegal camp built upon broken treaties with the Native Americans and nicknamed "Outlaw Camp," "Sin City," "Toughest City in the World," and "The Last Chinatown." Nonetheless, with entrepreneurial backup and advocacy provided by Deadwood mayor Sol Starr, Deadwood's Chinese community grew to over 250 residents and went on to build numerous emporiums, restaurants, laundries, and other service industries crucial to the infrastructure of Deadwood during its heyday in the late 1800s. Until, with similar boomtown speed, this fragile ecosystem, this miraculous diaspora, disappeared. Beginning in 1882, strict anti-immigration laws with Chinese-specific exclusion acts prevented the predominantly male population of Chinatown from marrying or bringing over wives and families, so that by the 1940s, the formerly thriving community had either died off or returned to China. By this time, the Chinese community had become so firmly integrated into Deadwood that celebration of Chinese holidays such as the Lunar New Year, for example, had become much-loved, blended community traditions. In 1991, in what now seems to you like a *haunting* memorial to Deadwood's significant Chinese history, Miss Kitty's Casino resurrected Deadwood's annual Chinese New Year celebrations—replete with firecrackers and lion dancers in ceremonial costume—a tradition that continued for twenty-one more years until the closing of Miss Kitty's in 2012.

8. Deadwood Derby

Even as Deadwood's Chinese New Year traditions fade yet again, roller derby's resurrection has made it all the way to the Black Hills and beyond. Upon your arrival in Deadwood, you're delighted to learn the Mountain Grand Casino will be hosting an exhibition bout during your stay to raise proceeds on behalf of the Wildlife Sanctuary in Spearfish. Maybe it's the one-too-many dirty martinis you drink in the casino bar while waiting for the bout to start, but your pictures turn out mostly as kinesthetic spangle, whirled blur, and whizzing loop. Still, you love the sense of speed, of ghostly afterimage, in these shots.

Your favorite derby girl at the exhibition bout is a rangy Native American blocker, Poca-Haunt Us. A registered member of the Karuk Tribe in California, Poca-Haunt Us skates during the regular derby season for the Coal Miners' Daughters out of Gillette, Wyoming—a team locally known for having raised thousands of dollars to support families in need, cancer research organizations, and other charities. According to Poca-Haunt Us's derby profile, she's a stay-at-home mother of two who enjoys Native American beadwork. She chose her derby jersey number of twenty-eight, she says, because it's a perfect number, and hopes her derby name, Poca-Haunt Us, will "bring out the inner bad ass native!"

9. Pigtail Loop

On your last day in Custer, you decide to drive the gorgeous but vertiginously treacherous Iron Mountain Road. Famous for its one-lane granite tunnels framing distant vistas of Mount Rushmore, as well as dizzying curlicues of spiraling pigtail bridges, Iron Mountain Road snakes through the mountain pass between Custer State Park and Keystone. There's not a lot that you find more intensely beautiful than mountain landscapes. But there's also nothing that makes you want to throw up or pass out more intensely than the sickening swirl of driving on the narrow outside ledge of a mountain's hairpin curve. You discovered this particular strain of acrophobia the hard way during the summer of 2010, at the summit of Yellowstone Park's Sylvan Pass, during a particularly memorable panic attack in which you sat down on the asphalt of a tiny pullout and ugly-cried, while considering the potential humiliation of having to be removed from the park by emergency helicopter. Since that meltdown, you've been working on a desensitization regimen, slowly attempting steeper and curvier mountain loops, switchback by switchback. The Iron Mountain Road drive couldn't be more beautiful: tangy turpentine scent of pine, russet granite outcroppings, extravagant manatees of clouds swimming in a hyperbole of blue. By the time you gingerly spiral around the summit and begin the final descent of loop-de-loop corkscrews in the three pigtail bridges near the eastern terminus by Keystone, you're practically giddy with adrenaline. Afterward, you drive to Hill City and eat an ice cream cone in the hot sun while your heartbeat slows. You consider getting a tattoo, but don't.

10. Recursive

Dusk on the Badlands Loop Road, heading home again, and as if on cue, the juvenile cottontail near Fossil Exhibit Trail freezes next to the scenic overlook's boardwalk. It's the same cottontail you've taken pictures of several times before on this trip. You recognize the distinctive triangular notch bitten out of the tip of one of its ears. This time, backlit by sunset, its thin-membraned ears begin to glow with the hot orange of tea lights behind glass. A car full of young Chinese tourists, joking with each other in Cantonese, all pause to take photographs of the cottontail with their iPhones. And for a brief moment, here is the cottontail, captured within the bright simultaneous frames of five iPhones, all lit up within the frame of your camera lens. Maybe you should have taken this picture, but you don't. Instead, you carry that image home with you—rabbit with its molten, lit-up ears glowing inside the iPhones glowing inside your Nikon—to unpack later like a Matryoshka doll.

Hall of Mirrors

1. Containment Culture

Recently, it's occurred to you that were the midcentury confessional women poets still alive, they'd be approximately the same age as your Japanese mother, a first-generation immigrant who eloped with your American father in 1955. Sylvia Plath and Anne Sexton were among the first poets you read and loved. Writing from the cloistered domestic enclaves of midcentury containment culture, with its resurgence of post–World War II cultural conservatism and Cold War paranoias about nuclear war, the poems of Plath and Sexton were like a radioactive leakage—a Cixousian seepage of female bodily fluids and breast milk, creating hairline fractures in the facade of midcentury white, middle-class conformity. Breaking frames, breaking silences, they raised questions that signaled to you the existence of possible loopholes, escape hatches, exit strategies from the oppressive and suffocating space you inhabited as a young person—a psychological landscape that was antithetical to your own survival as a person and as a poet.

The midcentury confessional poets offered you *glimmerings* of recognition from the frontlines of a battle for bodily autonomy: glimmerings that rigid gender roles were constructed and performative;

glimmerings that the idea of motherhood itself was constructed and performative; that there was a painful loss of self in the obligatory performance of or adherence to these rules and roles of genderhood and motherhood; and that autonomy and selfhood were inextricably related to the ability to make an informed *choice*.

You'd always felt that Sexton and Plath—intense, candid, transgressive—were far removed from your mother's world, yet in retrospect, there were striking commonalities. Your mother, like Sexton and Plath, suffered from mental illness (possibly borderline and/or narcissistic personality disorders), although unlike Sexton and Plath, your mother's mental illness was undiagnosed and untreated. Like Sexton and Plath, your mother had internalized the crushing obligations of Western beauty standards, as well as the culturally obligatory performances of gender and motherhood. Unlike Sexton and Plath, though, your mother didn't question these facades but instead ruthlessly disseminated, policed, and enforced them.

2. Doubled Images

Your mother liked to tell you that if you didn't have children, you wouldn't be "a real woman," that instead you'd be an "it." Yet parenting seemed to bring her little joy—only fury, resentment, disappointment. Outside of the house, though, she performed an elaboratively choreographed performance of motherhood, which she used to garner praise and acceptance. She made you complicit in these theatrics through costuming you in uncomfortable and impractical outfits and through scripting your conversations. Prior to taking you out in public she'd make you memorize coy phrases, replete with accompanying physical gestures, which she'd rehearse with you in advance. You learned early on that it was your job to manage your mother's moods, to bend over backward to keep her happy, to not contribute to her high blood pressure, which she insisted you'd "given" to her. Later in her life, with a candor brought on by the early stages of dementia, she'd obsessively recite her life's disappointments: marrying your father, coming to America, having you.

Of course, you immediately recognized the electric current of ambivalence and performativity running like a hot sizzling thread through the poems of Sexton and Plath. For you, these insights, these mirrorings, were thrilling. In both of these poets, you could see a liberatory struggle within the poems to locate a reflection of what Sexton often referred to as "the self's self."

In the second section of Anne Sexton's "The Double Image," for example, the first-person confessional speaker is released from the mental hospital into her mother's care following a suicide attempt after suffering from an acute episode of postpartum depression. The mother tells her daughter she cannot forgive her for attempting suicide, then blithely insists on having her daughter sit for a formal portrait. The insinuation seems to be that what the mother finds most *unforgivable* is the scandal, the breach of propriety. In section 3, when the mother is diagnosed with breast cancer, she claims the daughter has "given" it to her, and her "sweet hills"—representative of femininity and motherhood in Western culture—are "carved" out during surgery. Following her mastectomy, and leaving the hospital with a poor prognosis, the mother returns home, then has her own portrait painted.

Here, Sexton seems to allude to the ways in which *image*, or *appearance*, is privileged over the *real*—where obligatory performativity transcends actual lived experience, and midcentury womanhood and motherhood are posed, curated, and literally "contained" within the parameters of a frame. In section 6, mother and daughter portraits face off against one another, like mirror images ("my mocking mirror, my overthrown / love, my first image"), on opposite walls of the room. As the mother's health declines, the speaker likewise fails to thrive—trapped within the picture frame, suffocating within the stifling confines of midcentury gender roles: "I rot on the wall, my own / Dorian Gray." The poem culminates in the speaker's most fraught confession to her daughter Joy:

> I, who was never quite sure
> about being a girl, needed another
> life, another image to remind me.
> And this was my worst guilt; you could not cure
> nor soothe it. I made you to find me.

As the speaker becomes increasingly aware of maternal narcissism, codependency, the inability to be seen as an authentic self by her own mother, she realizes she has unconsciously replicated these same toxic enmeshments with her own daughter. And it is the candor of this realization that is illuminating, heartrending, and deeply troubling.

3. Like a Terrible Fish

You first realized your Japanese mother was suffering serious cognitive decline when she stopped recognizing herself in photographs, in mirrors. She'd become confused and irritated, asking, "Who that old man? What he doing there?" While you understood this to be one of the characteristic symptoms of dementia, it still made you wonder about selfhood, the nature of "the self's self." It seemed both painful and telling that when your mother perceived herself as being absent of stereotypical gender markers she found herself *unrecognizable*, and it also made you wonder about the foundational ways in which "femininity" is inextricably linked with youth.

Of course, these moments reminded you of Sylvia Plath's poem told from the point of view of a mirror, in which a woman "has drowned a young girl, and in me an old woman / Rises toward her day after day, like a terrible fish." In "The Mirror," the loss of self through death's encroachment seems almost secondary to the loss of self created by an inability to continue performing gender according to rules dictated by a white, cishet, abled, patriarchal gaze.

Yet, at the same time, who does the monstrous fish threaten exactly? The "young girl" has already drowned in the mirror's gaze, and the woman with her "tears and an agitation of hands" seems somewhat ineffectual, not someone who needs to be subdued by additional threat, or menace. Instead, she is searching the mirror to discover "what she really is"—in one sense, a quest for the self's self? And while the "terrible fish" that rises to the surface is potentially annihilating, the fish is also feral, monstrous, and undeniably powerful in comparison to the young girl and the woman. Monstrous enough, perhaps, to no longer be policed by an oppressive gaze. Monstrous enough to no longer have to perform for the "peanut-crunching crowd" alluded to in Plath's poem "Lady Lazarus."

4. Old Whore Petticoats

Any type of forced performance is undeniably oppressive in that it negates all aspects of bodily autonomy: the choice to be (or not to be) sexually inquisitive or sexually expressive; the choice to occupy the gender in which one feels most affirmed; the choice to love who and how one wishes to love; the choice to become, or not become, a mother; the choice to carry (or not carry) a fetus to term.

This sense of obligatory performativity was readily apparent in the jarring disconnection of Plath's various personas: the wholesome and breezy good-girl reportage in the letters home to her mother; the hypercompetitive, hyperbolic, and libidinally curious woman documented in the journals; the earthy, beekeeping domestic goddess, wife, and mother who performed this role so convincingly that critic A. Alvarez didn't even recognize Sylvia Hughes as being *the* Sylvia Plath whose poems he so admired when he came to dine at the Hugheses' house. Plath was once famously accused, by one of her college paramours, of being "all mask"—and yet the rigid obligations of gender roles, and the ways in which these obligations were at odds with both the intensity of her poetic ambitions and her struggles with mental illness, would seemingly make the social presentation of an "authentic" self exceedingly difficult.

Arguably, the most authentic presentation of self, despite also being the most painstakingly *constructed*, can be located in Plath's poems—perhaps because in their very theatricality, their self-consciousness regarding audience, and in their acknowledgment of their own performativity, they most transparently enact their own fraught subjectivities.

In Plath's work, there's an intense preoccupation with shedding away false selves to arrive at some furious, white-hot, incandescent core. (Maybe a discovery of the self's self?) Consider the New York clothes that are dropped out of the window of the Barbizon Hotel by protagonist Esther Greenwood in *The Bell Jar* for example. Or think of the delicately parenthetical "(My selves dissolving, old whore petticoats)— / To Paradise" at the end of "Fever 103." Similarly, in "Tulips," the speaker, who says she is "sick of baggage," relinquishes her belongings prior to surgery, as well as the markers of her *belonging*, which are also a kind of containment within the social order: "My patent leather overnight case like a black pillbox, / My husband and child smiling out of the family photo / Their smiles catch onto my skin, little smiling hooks." And in "Ariel," the speaker methodically peels away "dead hands, dead stringencies," mentally shaking off the child's cry that "melts in the wall" before stating that she is "the arrow / The dew that flies / Suicidal, at one with drive / Into the red / Eye, the cauldron of morning"—transforming herself into both a phallic weapon that will pierce the patriarchal gaze of the "peanut-crunching crowd," as well as into dew that will evaporate from the heat of the morning sun.

This process of shedding false selves is complex and multivalent. While the destruction or shedding of the old selves can be read as annihilative (death, destruction, or suicide), the core revelation is always also a kind of transformation, rebirth, or resurrection. Sometimes this rebirth renders the speaker too naked and vulnerable (an objectified/commodifiable female nude, an infantilized "pure gold baby / That melts to a shriek"), but in other instances, the resurrection generates something feral, monstrous, and powerful. Like the "terrible fish" rising in the mirror or a phoenix rising from the ashes. It evokes the monstrous feminine, who threatens the patriarchy, and, at the end of "Lady Lazarus," "eats men like air."

5. A Woman in the Shape of a Monster

It is depressing to think of how little systemic change has actually taken place since Sexton and Plath began writing about the complexities of gendered embodiment: the violence of attempting to articulate a female-identified subjectivity, the ambivalences and inequities of motherhood, the stigmas of mental illness. Writing at the nascence of the feminist movement, their poetry radically destabilized the rigidly conservative ethos of midcentury containment culture—creating hairline cracks in the foundations of the isolating silos that made up the mythos of the midcentury nuclear family.

Yet our contemporary late capitalist moment continues to deny subjectivity through controlling bodily autonomy and withholding physical/mental safety. It is an objectification, and a denial of personhood, that is anything *but* freedom. To be allowed to simply *be* in one's own body, to make choices about that body, to be the self's self, without harassment, violence, and interference, and to be allowed to do so with safety and dignity, should be the very basis of personhood. However, as evidenced by the overturning of *Roe v. Wade*, by the attacks on LGBTQIA+ communities, by the attacks on trans rights, by the ubiquity of mass shootings, by the shootings of unarmed Black and Indigenous people by police, by the attacks on Asian elders in the streets, by the attacks on higher education (especially the *humanities*), the act of occupying the self's self, the act of insisting on one's own subjectivity, is still coded as monstrous.

“A woman in the shape of a monster / a monster in the shape of a woman,” writes Adrienne Rich in the poem “Planetarium.” “The skies are full of them.” Perhaps as a poet, a contemporary of both Plath and Sexton, who was doubly marginalized through virtue of being both a woman and a lesbian, Rich was particularly attuned to both the difficulty and necessity of awakening into consciousness of the self's self. “I have been standing all my life in the / direct path of a battery of signals” she goes on to write in “Planetarium.” “I am an instrument in the shape / of a woman trying to translate pulsations / into images for the relief of the body / and the reconstruction of the mind.”

You return, once again, to Plath's “terrible fish”—emblematic of the monstrous feminine—the “terrible fish” that rises as the price for not performing, or being unable or unwilling to perform, as a commodified/commodifiable object.

Perhaps the self's self *is* the monster.

Perhaps the act of unmasking and meeting the mirrored gaze of the self's self is, in fact, subversively threatening to the point of inciting interference, control, and violence?

Perhaps the fish is “terrible” because it illuminates false social constructs and systemic oppressions, because it reveals the violent illusion/delusion of continuing to privilege a fragile, rapidly crumbling “center” as arbitrary, archaic, irrational, extractive, hegemonic, and—ultimately—*unsustainable.*

Scourge

1. Darkinfested

A cause of affliction or calamity, as in a plague, a bane, an infestation. A whip or a lash, to administer punishment or torture. The punisher that wields the lash. Although the whipping and lashing seems antiquated, the excoriating slice, sliver, and sting remain embedded in the idea of scourge.

Wasp nests simmering in attics, the itchy sizzle and thrum of agitated stripes, the secret secretions of bright satin-banded bodies breaking down the drywall into brittle sponge. A stained ceiling collapses in an explosion of rattle, wing, and drone.

The queasy slither and scatter of silverfish, smooth as the pearlescent glide of liquid eye shadow, when the light's snapped on at night in a damp room. Quietly chewing up the wallpaper and chewing their way through dusty books. Quietly writing their way through the cantos, making erasures in the canon.

You think of Lorine Niedecker's *darkinfested*. The secret, fearful, and destructive underbelly of the unconscious.

Glossy, orderly regiments of carpenter ants upholding their monarchy and their rigid caste systems.

Termites swarming and budding in ever-widening circles, like radio waves, around the pulsing, translucent, gelatinous signal of their queen.

Police officers encased in the shiny carapace of riot gear, spilling like weevils or deathwatch beetles, into the streets of Ferguson, Missouri.

You think of Lorine Niedecker's *darkinfested.*

2. Excessive Force

In an episode titled "Hero," from the first season of *Angel*, the spin-off series to *Buffy the Vampire Slayer*, the Scourge is a fascistic militant group of full-blood demons seeking to eradicate mixed-blood demons. They murder adults and children alike with ruthless precision, the menacing rhythmic jog of their boots on pavement driving mixed-blood demons into hiding. Throughout the episode, the Scourge pursue a peaceful group of humanoid mixed-blood demons called the Listers, intent on exterminating the Listers through use of the Beacon—their newly invented death machine that identifies and annihilates all mixed-blood demons with a killing light. The Scourge is foiled, but only when Doyle—a beloved and central character in the narrative—makes the ultimate heroic sacrifice to save the Listers.

Like the Marauders, who attempt to exterminate the Morlocks, an outcast group of mutants in the X-men Universe. The Morlocks named themselves after the subterranean alien race in H. G. Wells's *The Time Machine*, and because their marked physical differences make them so vulnerable to terrible hegemonies (including medical experimentation), they choose to segregate themselves and live underground.

Like the fascistic terrorist organization, Hydra ("Hail Hydra! Cut off a limb, and two more shall take its place!"), from the Marvel Universe, attempting to initiate a new and malevolent world order through the invention and deployment of various weapons of mass destruction such as the Betatron Bomb, the Overkill Horn (capable of simultaneously detonating all nuclear weapons worldwide by remote), or the bioengineered Death-Spore Bomb.

Like the metallic drumming rattle and clank of Stormtroopers clattering through the decks of the Death Star, Darth Vader's massive imperial space station armed with the "ultimate weapon"—a superlaser capable of decimating an entire planet with one strike.

Like the Sentinels, the giant mutant-hunting robots programmed to detect and exterminate mutants in the X-men.

Like Galactus, the most-feared being in the Marvel Universe—a ravenous devourer of worlds, capable of shoving a straw deep inside a planet and sucking it dry as if it were a puny, crumpling juicebox.

3. Nonindigenous

Colonization by alien species is, of course, a central trope of science fiction but has always/already occurred, and continues to occur, in both our human history and our planetary ecology. Much like H. G. Wells's Martian "red weed" from *The War of the Worlds*, or the fuzzy, cutely cooing, and exponentially asexually reproducing tribbles (*Polygeminus grex*) from *Star Trek*, non-native invasive species repeatedly wreak brutal cultural and environmental havoc—frequently to the point of extinguishing indigenous species.

The tumbleweed, for example, long considered to be an emblematic semiotic icon for the visual landscape of the American West, is not even native to the continent. Actually a Siberian alien thistle, native to the steppes of the Ural Mountains in Russia, the tumbleweed's first reported appearance in the United States took place in Bon Homme County, South Dakota, in 1877. Thought to have been accidentally imported in a shipment of flax seed from the Ukraine, the thistle—which exploits damaged native ecosystems—ran rampant over prairie grasslands damaged by farming. A single tumbleweed can disseminate as many as 250,000 seeds—each seed a tightly coiled embryo of a new tumbleweed plant—and by 1900, the Russian thistle, also sometimes referred to as a "wind witch," had tumbleweeded all the way west to the Pacific Coast.

In June, all along the banks of the Vermillion River in Vermillion, South Dakota, there's a gorgeous profusion of purple as musk thistles (*Carduus nutans*) blaze into bloom. A member of the sunflower (Asteraceae) family and native to Europe, central Asia, and East Africa, the hyperbolic red-violet flowers are thrust from a crown of spikes like tight hot clusters of fireworks. Their heads are so heavy they droop on their spiny stems, earning them the nickname "nodding thistle." Like the tumbleweed, musk thistles invade disturbed soil areas: floodplains, stream banks, pastures, rangeland, roadsides, and waste areas. A single plant can produce up to 120,000 seeds, which are dispersed by wind and can remain viable in the soil for as long as ten years—making this colonizer preternaturally hardy and difficult to manage, let alone eradicate, even with herbicides.

Known as "the vine that ate the South," kudzu was first introduced to the United States in 1876, as part of a Japanese exhibition garden at the Centennial Exposition in Philadelphia, Pennsylvania. During the Great Depression, kudzu was promoted as a promising solution to soil erosion and planted en masse by the Civilian Conservation Corps, as well as by local farmers, throughout the 1930s and 1940s. In its native Asia, kudzu was beloved for centuries both as a food source as well as a medicinal ingredient. Without its indigenous Asian insect predators, however, and in the climate of the American South, kudzu grew and flourished at an unexpectedly phenomenal rate. Kudzu vines have been known to grow as much as a foot a day during the summer months, and up to sixty feet a year. It is unusually resilient to herbicides. Over seven million acres of the Deep South are now covered in kudzu, and the USDA reclassified it as a noxious weed in 1972.

4. Scour

Even though the etymological roots are unrelated, the word "scourge" makes you think of the word "scour": the metallic swish of steel wool ringing against metal like a weird singing bowl, sand scouring a steel pan, drought and wind and overcultivated topsoil scouring the Great Plains's 1930's Dust Bowl into gritty black and white.

As a child, you found the anthropomorphized bubbles in the Dow Scrubbing Bubbles commercials vaguely upsetting. They were somehow too aggressively blue, too bug-eyed and blinky, too bristly on the bottom, too zealous in their frenetic declarations that "We do the work so you don't have to!" The ringleader bubble, who eventually went on to be named Scrubby and would narrate recent findings by "scrubologists," was, during the commercials of your childhood, voice acted by the same actor who did the voice of Tigger in the Winnie-the-Pooh cartoons. You found it deeply unsettling that these freakishly manic scrubbing bubbles were all being washed down the drains of sinks and bathtubs, flushed down toilets, and swept away to fizzle and blink, to sing their songs of scouring deep in the belly of the city's sewer systems.

Dow Scrubbing Bubbles, manufactured by Dow Chemicals, before being sold to S.C. Johnson in 1997.

5. The Dao of Scour(ge):

Napalm B
Agent Orange
Rocky Flats
Organophosphates
Chlorpyrifos
Bhopal
Lorsban

6. Abschied

There's an overview in town at the top of the bluffs in Vermillion called Firefly Alley, stretching all the way down into the river valley, with patches of farmland in the distance. On June nights, it's all phosphorescent glitter and glitz, a discotheque of absinthe-green twinkle lights. Only each year, there are fewer fireflies in this bioluminescent light show of candela, lambert, and luciferin. Tiny green stars blinking out one by one.

In Franz Joseph Haydn's Symphony 45 in F-sharp Minor, also known as the "Farewell" Symphony, the fourth-movement presto finale anomalously and abruptly shifts into a poignant adagio, and bit by bit, various instruments from the orchestra gradually fall away until the symphony concludes with two solo violins playing a simple duet in counterpoint. In the original summer 1772 staging of the symphony, premiered in the Esterháza palace on the Hungarian plains, as each instrumental line concluded its part in the symphony, the musicians blew out the candles on their music stands, one by one, and quietly exited the stage—leaving only the two solo violinists and the concert master on a barely lit stage for the finale.

Abschied.

Scour.

(Honeybees with shattered nervous systems. Honeybees with memory loss. Honeybees with impaired olfactory learning.)

Scourge.

darkinfested

Writing Down the Bones

1. Desperately Seeking Tsunami

Oysterville, Washington, almost at the end of Long Beach Peninsula, is across the Columbia River from Astoria, Oregon. Long Beach Peninsula is a slender finger between the Pacific Ocean and Willapa Bay, stretching from Cape Disappointment State Park at the base, to Ledbetter Point State Park at the tip. Oysterville is past McGowan, past Chinook, past Ilwaco, Holman, Seaview, Long Beach, Oceanside, and Ocean Park. You've come to do a monthlong residency along with five other artists. Your plan is to work on a new manuscript of poems commemorating the 2011 Tohoku earthquake and tsunami in Japan. You're seeking out tsunami's stomping grounds, and the Tsunami Evacuation signs along the peninsula, dotted with bright patches of cranberry bogs, let you know that you've come to the right place to explore her habitat, to feel close to her haunting power.

2. Sea Lion

There's a dead sea lion on the beach, and the sculptor covets its bones. All of the women residents eagerly want to see, and so plans are made for a field trip. The sea lion is immense, partially decomposed, and initially camouflaged by sand. Up close, it's all sable gray skin, wrinkled fat, and bone—mottled with a strange oil-slick bruise in hues of indigo blue and deep red. The *idea* of a sea lion, rendered as vulnerably inanimate flesh in sand like a Chaim Soutine painting. But this is no still life. There are clouds of flies and pearly grains of maggots. The smell hangs like a heavy rancid grease in the salted air and even when one stays downwind and is careful not to breathe in, it clings to the back of the tongue with a fiercely invasive afterlife.

With purple rubber gloves, a garden trowel, and shears, the sculptor—with the help of the other poet—liberates the bones from flesh, and they are all shadow, architecture, and light: the tunneled complex hollows of vertebrae, the paired mandibles tipped with a fierce triangular tooth, the pubis bone shaped like a large blank eye.

You take photographs. The pen-and-ink artist watches closely for a while, then walks further down the shoreline to stare at the sea.

3. Bear

There's a sense of being alternately terrified and hopeful about seeing bears, who are starting to come out of hibernation, and who have been rumored to appear on the property. The garbage is thrillingly locked in a bear-proof shack, and all the residents are captivated by stories of bears appearing in the backyard outside of the floor-length windows. However, when Chef Darice suggests that the sculptor move the buckets filled with soaking sea lion bones further away from the cabins and dining hall, everyone agrees that this seems like a good idea.

4. Doc's Tavern / Jack's Mercantile

The nearest town to Oysterville, which is mostly historic village, is Ocean Park, a few miles down the peninsula. Ocean Park is home to Jack's Mercantile, which is located "at the light" in Ocean Park. A "purveyor of fine goods since 1885," Jack's sells groceries, hardware, and general merchandise, including a wide range of clamming equipment. Particularly fascinating are the clam guns, which come in four price ranges based on materials and relative fanciness: PVC, aluminum, stainless steel, and stainless steel with vacuum release. Of course, you secretly want a clam gun.

Also located in Ocean Park is Doc's Tavern, the exterior of which alluringly promises shuffleboard! And darts! And pool! Clearly, it's a dive bar of the best sort and the source of much conjecture. One Google reviewer scathingly calls it a "jankey bar" with the "worst food and service ever," which only seems to fuel the fire. An outing finally comes together late in the residency, and it's more than possibly hoped for. The ceiling is garnished with a snarling, taxidermied bear rug and there are good local drafts, rubber-booted locals, and pull-tabs behind the bar. The residents are almost sad not to have come earlier. In the bathroom, a nice young woman introduces herself to you and asks where you're visiting from. She marvels that you're all the way from South Dakota, wants to know what it's like there. Sort of like Ocean Park, you tell her, but without the ocean.

5. Glamming

Several times during the residency, rubber boots are assembled and loaned out to the residents, and Jeff, the residency manager, takes everyone clamming during ebb tide. You walk all the way out into the drained bay with buckets and hoe through the sand, feeling and listening for the ceramic clink of porcelain-like shell against metal claw-tooth. The oyster lines are exposed, and shorebirds swirl on the horizon in tornadic whorls. There are tiny Dungeness crabs who make threatening postures with their pincers. It is very peaceful to dig in the cool wet sand, to hear the satisfying clunk of clams dropped in the bucket.

The clams add up surprisingly quickly. Jeff rinses them in the clam sink outside his house, and en masse, they are beautiful.

Cream-colored shells swirled and mottled with brown patterns and freckles. Occasionally, one marked in the deep pansy purplish-blue of mimeograph carbons.

After being rinsed off, the clams are set in buckets of clean seawater to purge for a day or so—spitting out and expelling the grit from their shells. Darice fries them up for dinner, and they are absolutely delicious.

One night, the residents make fun of "glampers" until you realize that technically, Jeff hasn't been taking the residents clamming but rather *glamming*.

6. Herschel, the Sea Lion

Returning from her weekend, Chef Darice reports an excitement on the peninsula. Her friends had a sea lion in their front yard! Darice and her husband are called to come and see, and the local sheriff is called as well. When the sheriff arrives, he attempts to shoo the sea lion from the yard, and when the sea lion *galoomphs* out into the road, he shoos it safely across the intersection, at which point the sea lion becomes tired and hides behind a tree. The sheriff says it's become an increasingly common occurrence. Apparently, some sea lions have figured out that instead of swimming all the way around the lengthy tip of the peninsula, they can more quickly move from ocean to bay and vice versa by using the slender width of peninsular land as a bridge.

Sea lions are apparently playful, social, adaptable, and highly intelligent. Beloved by tourists and locals alike, they have also become the scourge of the salmon and sports fishing industries, due to their gleefully insatiable and ruthless poaching of salmon. In fact, salmon populations have been regularly decimated by incorrigible sea lions that have learned to gorge themselves on vulnerable salmon moving upstream at major Pacific Northwest dams such as the Ballard Locks near Seattle or Oregon's Bonneville Dam on the Columbia

River. Dwindling salmon stock is a viable concern, yet sea lions are a protected species, leading to increasingly intricate games of cat and mouse between sea lions and Oregon/Washington Departments of Fish and Wildlife. Some of the most notorious of the sea lions have become minor celebrities of sorts, and are named—Herschel, Hondo, Spot, Fang, C319. They can jump over six-foot gates to dam orifices. They're apparently resistant to the deployment of fake killer whales, rubber bullets, and hazing by firecrackers. They manage to swim back to the dams even after they've been removed far downstream. They've been known to return even after having been deported all the way to Mexico.

These Fatty McFattersons, occasionally stuffing themselves to well over one thousand pounds, are simply doing what sea lions do, and it's easy to root for their cleverness—even in the face of endangered salmon runs—given that the dams, which are man-made, are the original creators of the impasse.

7. Foot Bones

About a year after the 2011 Japanese tsunami, debris from the tsunami that had been swept into the Pacific gyre began washing up along the Pacific coastline: soccer balls, motorcycles, air freshener. Most disturbing were the buoyant tennis shoes filled with foot bones.

8. Elk Bone Cemetery

One afternoon, Cyndy Hayward, the founder of Willapa Bay AiR, takes the residents on a walk to see the elk boneyard. You walk along the bayside, past the old Oysterville cannery, by the improvised found folk-art sculptures, and down a winding path to a man-made ditch. The group is accompanied by Miles, Cyndy's white standard poodle, who is all floppy ears and friendly intelligence—extravagant and unlikely as a unicorn. Most of the residents have left pets at home and shamelessly vie for Miles's attention whenever he's around. At the elk boneyard, there are elk bones, skulls, and lacey frills of nasal cartilage. The skulls, in particular, are especially gorgeous. The sculptor brings some back to her studio for further study.

9. Mollusk without a Shell

Although you never actually get to see a bear, there are many other animals: eagle, deer, shorebirds, gulls, crabs, a red-striped garter snake, tiny green frogs the size of a thumbnail striped with bright yellow piping, a tubby chocolate lab who sleeps in the middle of the road.

And oh! How the rain brings out a space-alien menagerie of slugs and snails! Dark slugs like soft, black figs. (*Arion ater.*) Microscopically tiny snails that could fit inside a doll's teacup, ranging to snails with shells the size of silver dollars: chocolate brown, with flashes of orange and a helixing beige, snake-skinned pattern. (*Arianta arbustorum.*) The language of snail anatomy is likewise beautiful: heliciform, umbilicus, columellar, aperture, sinistral, dextral.

The strangest and most majestic, however, are the Pacific banana slugs. Growing from seven to ten inches when they reach full size, these gentle giants range in color from bright ochre yellow to various types of browns and greens. Occasionally, they are leopard spotted. Slime shimmered at night, moving with the muscular pulse of earthworms, they are the stuff of science fiction with their cleverly inquisitive antennae, their undulating keels, and their caudal mucus pores known as pneumostomes—not to mention their notorious habit of gnawing off their partners' penis after copulation.

Of course, you love them. Your root metaphor for becoming vulnerable, raw, and anxious is to feel like *a mollusk without a shell*, and so they are a totemic emotional animal for you. You confess that one night you couldn't resist and took one back to your studio for a while to observe up close and take pictures. With a pale greenish-brown body and a bright yellow mantle, it was—fully extended—over seven inches long, cool and sticky as a peeled refrigerated kiwi. It was gentle, and curious, and so *unlikely*. And when you returned it to the wet dark, it seemed like a surreal dream you'd had, except for the pictures on Facebook, which were met with a combination of delight and trepidation.

10. Made Flesh

Over the chain-linked vertebrae of a month's worth of these easy days—sandwiched on the peninsula between the beauties of the ocean and the bay, spoiled with delicious food, and within a lovely community of other artists—a book easily fleshes itself out. It is seemingly magic, this transubstantiation: tsunami, her superhero nemeses, the feral trauma and circadian rhythms of the tide. It is a strangely fleeting time, yet beautifully substantial. It is—there is no other way to say it—an unexpected manifestation, an enormous oceanic gift.

Swarm

1. A Knot of Snakes

Swarm sounds like warm with the serpentine arabesque of a hiss spiraling around the word. Like the heat-sleepy tangled knot work of baby garter snakes languorously coiling and uncoiling—corded shoelaces tying and untying themselves on a sunbaked concrete sidewalk.

The hiss a slight edge surrounding the protective bubble of communion to those held within the collective safety of the swarm.

Swarm rhymes with warn, as if to convey a sense of threat—think of the 1978 sci-fi disaster movie *The Swarm* starring Michael Caine and Katherine Ross, in which a swarm of deadly African bees terrorizes American cities. But it also sounds like sworn, as if to convey agency, intent, determination.

2. A Wake of Turkey Vultures

Late summer afternoon and turkey vultures parabola the water tower in Vermilliion, South Dakota, off downtown's Main Street, casting smooth shadows on concrete like sleek, dark fish. They like to catch the updrafts from the river bluffs to kettle and roost in the old water tower—sometimes aggregating into a swarm of as many as sixty or seventy at a time. Some Vermillionaires find the turkey vultures off-putting—what with their carrion-hungry ways, their featherless and slightly grizzled red-fleshed heads, and their—let's be honest about this—frankly *disgusting* defense mechanism of vomiting up toxic stomach acids when threatened. But when they fly, they're aerodynamically majestic—long-feathered dihedrals, silver shimmer of secondary feathers.

Maybe it's because you're half Japanese, but you adore large aggregations of animals—particularly when they intersect interestingly with humans. You're charmed by the miniature spotted Sika deer in Nara, Japan, for example, that have overrun the park and taken over the streets of the city—stalling traffic, lounging on the sidewalks, appropriating sandwiches from tourists, and nuzzling through purses and pockets for potential treats. Once considered sacred, the deer are nationally protected, and although increasingly aggro to the point of being rude about food, most have learned to bow after receiving (or stealing) a treat.

In addition to Nara Park, Japan is also home to eleven "cat islands" overrun by roving armies of cats, the most famous of which, Aoshima, seems to be aswirl with marmalade tabbies. Or there's Zao Fox Village in the Miyagi Prefecture, which is sanctuary to over six species of friendly, very clever, and very mischievous foxes. Not to mention Okushima, Japan's rabbit island, where visitors can tour a defunct mustard gas factory prior to being swarmed by hordes of gregarious bunnies. In a popular Facebook meme, a young Japanese woman is shown running down a path while being chased by a seemingly infinite mob of exceedingly enthusiastic rabbits!

And so when the local newspaper, the *Vermillion Plain Talk*, reports that a new, smoothly bulbous water tower is being built over by the Walmart Supercenter, you're quick to sign the Save the Old Vermillion Water Tower petition, not only because the water tower's over one hundred years old and interesting from a historical preservation standpoint but because you love the swarms of turkey vultures that come to roost on the old water tower. Maybe a turkey vulture roost is not as cute, or *kawaii*, as an island of rabbits or a fox sanctuary, but still . . . perhaps in time it could become its own quirky local attraction?

3. A Pod of Walruses

Unusual aggregations of animals can also sometimes function as a warning of ecological imbalance. When a massive swarm of walruses—over thirty-five thousand of them—began congregating on the beaches of a barrier island near Point Lay in northwest Alaska, the National Oceanic and Atmospheric Administration warned that this anomalous haul out was due to loss of sea ice in offshore areas, serving as yet another harbinger of rapid global warming and climate change.

The aerial photographs of the walruses swarming the beach are stunningly disturbing—the sand completely covered in a jostling portly corpulence of throbbing walrus flesh, punctuated by pair after pair of dangerous ivory tusks. Not surprisingly, numerous walrus corpses were left behind, their deaths apparently caused by the stampede.

4. A Fever of Stingrays

From the air, like flickering chips of Formica, from below, a swarm of Pokémon-cute anime smiley faces—their bodies mimicking softly undulant waves. Or sometimes winging their pectoral fins like birds—fin tips flicking through the surface of the water like the up-flipped triangular corners of galette dough.

The movement too cool and smooth to evoke a fever, and so the group name must be because of the serrated barbs on their tails that lash up and release venom when stingrays are surprised or startled from above. Symptoms for stingray envenomation include:

diaphoresis, nausea, cardiac arrhythmias, tremors, skin rash, headache, delirium, fever, hypertension, syncope, anxiety.

In poetry circles, the names for groups of animals in the "a _________ of _________" construction has perhaps become somewhat outré, if not downright clichéd. But still! *A fever of stingrays*! Maybe it's now your most-favorite-ever group name for animals. Followed closely by a conspiracy of lemurs, which sounds like it should be the name of an art-rock noise band.

(If you Google conspiracy of lemurs, photographs of lemurs nested and stacked next to and on top of one another come up, gazing at the camera with their strikingly intense, black pupil-studded amber eyes. Their tails are very pleasingly *stripy*.)

You once lived with a lover who was shy and withdrawn in public but hilariously gregarious in private. He was clever with accents and could do hysterical impersonations of celebrities and cartoon characters. Sometimes he'd pretend to be *The Crocodile Hunter*'s Steve Irwin, dangling one of your cats, stripy tales swishing, over a pretend crocodile. "Crikey!" he'd exclaim. "What a beauty! Let's feed it some *chicken*!"

Steve Irwin died in 2006 in a freak stingray accident, when he startled an Australian bull ray from above while snorkeling. Stingrays typically like to camouflage themselves in the sand—alert to the natural electrical charges of their potential prey with electrical sensors around their mouths called *ampullae of Lorenzini*. You feel like this is a ridiculously beautiful name for electrical sensors.

Where are you even going with this? You're not sure. Maybe it's that the swarm of neurons startled by a fight-or-flight response can make even a gentle, camouflaging creature lash out with a barb to the heart. Maybe it's that to swim in a fever of stingrays could be quite beautiful, and not as dangerous as stepping on one. Maybe it's that you secretly covet *ampullae of Lorenzini*.

5. Hive Mind

At first, in the YouTube meme circulating on Facebook, it appears to be a large grayish snake slowly making its way across a sidewalk. But on second glance, it's much too translucent to be a snake, and something isn't right in the way it moves—too slow, too much of a pulsing. It moves like a gigantic worm. Then the shock of the video camera zooming in to reveal that the gargantuan worm is made up of hundreds of tiny, noodle-shiny larvae, collaborating to migrate in unison. Like a roving metanarrative. Like an aggregation of metadata.

Further Googling reveals that the ribbonlike mass is made up of darkwinged fungus gnat larvae. Entomologists don't understand the aggregating behavior of the larvae, but they are apparently considered useful pests in both greenhouses and mushroom cellars. Harmless, even beneficial, yet the spectacle nonetheless both fascinates and unnerves. Much like the viral meme of the male seahorse *fwoofing* out clouds of tiny white baby seahorses from his abdomen—like a series of sneezes expelling clouds of rhinoviruses.

How much of the world organizes, or patterns itself, using an Ouroboros-like feedback loop? The epically spiraling tornadic whorls of starlings in a murmuration, the dark cloud of gnats, a cluster of shorebirds scooting low over the water like a black-and-white silk scarf turning itself inside out, and the schooling behavior of fish all potentially reveal a universal self-organizing process of attraction, repulsion, alignment, and searching by which a single organism functions collaboratively within the aggregate. Interestingly, this same self-organizing feedback loop may also determine how individual cells adapt themselves to environment-specific conditions.

How much of one thing mirrors another? Apparently, the behavior of honeybee colonies mimics the behavior of neurons in primate brains when it comes to decision-making processes, such as scouting out, establishing a quorum, and then relocating to a new nest site. For example, scout bees perform waggle dances to introduce input about desirable nest sites, while sender scout bees (responsible for coordinating the move to the new nest site) send "stop signals" to the waggle dancers by tapping them on the head and emitting a short buzz. These "stop signals" function analogously to cross-inhibition signals in primate brains—thereby allowing neurons to weigh input from, compare, and select from different alternatives before establishing a quorum and arriving at a decision.

Attraction, repulsion, alignment, searching. How do we swarm, search, flock, murmur, pod, clat, wake, knot, squirm, and fever in our virtual apiaries and aviaries of social networks such as Facebook and Twitter?

How much of the world organizes, or patterns itself, using an Ouroboros-like feedback loop?

How much of one thing mirrors another?

Even now, your neurons flocking to this and attracted to that.

Swarm of honeybees seeking out a new meme . . .

Home(r) Sweet Home(r)

1. Moose

On the first night of your residency at the Bunnell Arts Center in Homer, Alaska, on the way back from dinner with the Arts Center directors, you pass two moose gangling about in someone's front yard! Two calves, although you privately like to think of them as *mooslings*: woolly and damp in fog and headlights, all knobby knees, leafy ears, high haunched, with soft wet noses, glamorous eyelashes.

There's the magical collective indrawn breath of Elizabeth Bishop's blue, dented enamel bus, released only after the moose calves pause for a moment, to gaze back at us in curiosity—"grand, otherworldy"—before clattering away. "Why, why do we feel / (we all feel) this sweet / sensation of joy?"

2. Patchwork

The other artist in residence at the Bunnell Arts Center is textile artist Abigail Kokai. She's piecing together a community quilt. In collaboration with Homer residents, she holds workshops where people create panels—stories and images about their lives in Homer—interspersed with panels she makes herself based on her local observations and interactions. Community members also bring in fabrics to donate: clothes, scraps, and other cloth materials. The panels are assembled like collages in textile: elaborately ornamented, embroidered, richly graphic, and frequently accompanied by narrative text. Each panel tells a particular story, or captures a specific local moment, and the cumulative effect is like a graphic memoir rendered in textiles. Abigail is quiet—an intent listener—with a calm open face and an easy smile. "Bee tee dubs," she likes to say, as she shares tips for delicious things to eat or interesting things to see. You hear her sewing machine whirring late into the night in the gallery below your room. Her quilts are absolutely stunning.

3. Cranes

The sandhills have landed in Homer, Alaska, filling the air with their hollow wood-block burbled warbling, and dancing their fan dances of courtship in Beluga Slough. Late evenings, you come to watch them parachuting in. They are a paradox of simultaneous grace and ungainliness. One moment long-necked aerialists, embodying the iconic lines of traditional Japanese wood-block prints. The next, skinny-legged pear-bottomed tourists hang gliding in for a flat-footed landing. They delicately pick their way through the slough—feeding or making their scarlet-capped courtship displays to one another. They're a little bit uncanny, with their gold eyes and iron-rusted gray feathers that pick up the light as if they've been dredged in gilt. When they extend their necks into the air, tilt their heads back and trumpet, they are like strange ornithological irises, calling down the setting sun. When they fly against the backdrop of snow-capped peaks and frothing turquoise ocean, they are magnificent.

4. John Cage

In Homer, the scenery is so epic that one instinctively spends one's time looking up at mountains, clouds, and birds or looking out at oceanic horizons, the slow motion of boats, or the way morning light silvers wet ebb-tide sand into a glistening sheet of tin foil. One day, though, you spend your time looking down at the small improvisations, the accidental still lifes, of seaweed, shells, and stones, and you become lost in it: here, a spill of clam shells like a broken scattering of eggshells; here, a large white shell like a broken tea cup splattered with flecks of marigold yellow; here, a dead crab; here, an unhinged shell like a porcelain bathtub partially filled with sand; here, the pattern of ebb-tide sand like modernist hands holding one another. All of this swept away by the tide like a Tibetan sandpainting. All of this visual music random and aleatoric, like a John Cage composition.

5. Eagle

There's a bald eagle that makes regular triangulations from the western side of Bishop's Beach to the northernmost point of Beluga Slough, back to a stand of trees on the eastern side of Bishop's Beach. She scatters the ducks and makes the dogs bark. Her call—repeated, pealed axe strikes of sound that are both hair-raisingly electric and unexpectedly *chirpy*—echoes all the way down the length of the beach. At night you study your photographs of her, admiring the muscular bellows of her wings, the aerodynamic tuck of her feet, the bright waxy yellow of her beak.

6. Snakebitch

It is the day you get called a "Snakebitch" on the internet, and fog pours in from the bay like glorious horror movie fog, or cheesy rock band fog-machine fog. First it rolls off the mountains in Kachemak Bay State Park until they disappear and then fills up the bay until you can no longer see the water. Bit by bit, it climbs up the hill in Homer, until everything's a chamber of cloud and mist. Soon the rain comes down in cold sheets, and after you've finished writing for the day, you console yourself by streaming *Daredevil* on Netflix while sampling Alaskan craft beer: Galaxy Brewing Company's White IPA and a Belgian dark ale by Midnight Sun Brewing Company called Monk's Mistress.

Snakebitch.

Snakebitch!

7. Raven

One afternoon, as you're walking downtown, you're buzzed by a raven. *Caw, caw, caw* and the *fwoomp fwoomp fwoomp* of glossed wings dive-bombing your head. You're initially charmed, but your bemusement soon turns to alarm when he does it again. And then again. You're ducking and bobbing each time you're startled by one of his aggressive swoops, and you're sure it makes for a pretty strange sight. You imagine the headline: "Visiting South Dakotan Harassed by Raven on Pioneer Avenue." Finally, it occurs to you that maybe he's after something shiny, and so you remove the octopus clip with sparkly accents that's holding up your hair, and he stops. You call him a *Naughty Monkey*. You wonder if it's the same raven you saw the week before, further along on the same street, pissing off a mother eagle by swooping around the nest that you discovered, through your zoom lens, was filled with fuzzy eaglet chicks.

8. The Yurt Workers

You're invited to go on a boat ride to deliver a tarp to the Tutka Bay yurt being set up for summer stays in the Kachemak Bay State Park. The yurts are round tentlike structures with wood latticework that house sleeping platforms, a fire stove, propane burner, bear-proof food lockers, with a freestanding outhouse less than one hundred feet away. The yurt locations have marvelous names like China Poot, Haystack Beach, and Humpy Creek and are strategically located near state park trailheads, as well as kayaking, clamming, and fishing sites. They can be rented by the night by parties of up to six people during the summer months. The day is overcast and cool, the bay like silvered glass. Occasionally, sea otters cock up their quizzical heads and lift up their paddled feet from the water like strange beings rising out of a mirror. There are two dogs on board. One of them is a tiny black lab puppy, and after peeing on the floor, he settles in for the ride, and the passengers take turns holding him. When the temperature drops further into the bay, he begins to shiver, and so you zip him up inside your vest, where he sleeps. The yurt workers ride back to Homer afterward, and they fill the boat with the scent of damp wool and pine. One of them shyly shows you a picture on his phone of spring wildflowers from the trail.

9. The Homer Spit

A narrow finger of land extending 4.5 miles into Kachemak Bay, the southernmost end of the Homer Spit also marks the end of the U.S. highway system. The site of the City of Homer Port & Harbor, the spit is busy with incoming and outgoing fishing boats (Homer is known as the Halibut Fishing Capitol of the World), pleasure boats, and water taxis and lined with restaurants and shops, many of which are geared toward summer tourists.

The historic Salty Dawg Saloon is located near the end of the spit—an old log cabin structure topped off with an iconic lighthouse tower. The cabin was one of the original cabins built on the Homer town site in 1897 and served as the first post office, a railroad station, a grocery store, and a coal mining office before eventually becoming the Salty Dawg Saloon in 1957.

Inside, the bar is famously plastered with signed dollar bills. In the ladies' room, there are free rainbow condoms available on the mirror above the sink, courtesy of a local health clinic. Someone has drawn an arrow pointing to the condoms, with a note in magic marker that reads:

Nurse <3 Molly says, "Wash your Hands!" & "Have Safe Sex"

In pink marker, someone else recommends:

Please take "2" & double bag it—never know where it's been!

Followed by an editorial note in black marker:

NEVER wear two condoms at once . . . the latex will rub together and BREAK! One will do it!   True story.

10. Tsunami Siren

During your two weeks in Homer, you've been working furiously on tsunami poems. You are in her territory. There are multiple tsunami sirens in Homer, like giant, spiral CFL (compact fluorescent lights) energy-saving light bulbs.

You're startled one Wednesday afternoon, when the tsunami siren suddenly emits a series of tones, followed by a gigantic, hand-of-God voice ringing across the beach, saying: "This is a test of the Kenai Peninsula Borough Early Warning System. This is only a test. If this were an actual emergency, you would be instructed to tune in to your local radio station. This is only a test."

Every time you drive back into town from the spit, you see the same large bald eagle, comfortably roosting on top of the tsunami siren.

"Oh, he likes it up there," someone tells you when you ask about it.

It seems like a sign. You think of the semiotics of home, and homing. Of the way an eagle likes to return to a familiar roost. Of how a tsunami can be called in to landing by the siren calls of certain coasts. Of how a place that is not home, can sometimes feel, for a short time, like home.

Meditations on an Emergency

In the stunned fallout after the 2016 election, a friend posts an article to your Facebook wall about how artists need to be the first responders in our postelection America, and you think, *yes*. Because—amid a rising tide of graffitied swastikas, hate crimes, climate change denying, and a veritable tsunami of disaster capitalism—it *is* an *emergency*. This needless teetering on the cusp of global catastrophe. And because you truly believe in art as a field of possibility and potential. As a site of radical empathy. As a place to enact and articulate the unconscious, the instinctive, the *unsayable*. And so *yes*. But how to turn letters and text and code into a tsunami warning system? How to semaphore, with language, the exhortatory swirl of flashing red lights? How to find the words to set the sirens *howling*?

◎

Since the election, you've been choosing to share your most raw, personal work at readings. The poems about racism, about being bullied as a biracial child growing up in Wyoming; the poems about sexual and physical abuse; the story about the time you and your lover were nearly queer-bashed; the piece about the drunken man who broke down your door and beat you until the police arrived; the essay about trauma, workplace misogyny, and the taboo of female *rage*. You do this in spite of the queasiness of making yourself too vulnerable in uncertain public spaces. You do this in spite of the stern internal editorial voice that's constantly warning against solipsism. You do this in solidarity. You do this because the personal *is still* political. You do this because you are angry, and you are sick of silencing yourself, and you are even sicker of being silenced, and sicker still at the thought of others being silenced. You do this as an act of courage and to join the other voices you hear speaking up with a kind of clarity and strength that you find inspiring. You do this to hold space so that other voices may be inspired to speak their truths as well. You imagine song—feral, chipped, gorgeous, and wild—rising up like a tornado swirl of starlings to blot out the white static of silence, of complicity.

◎

The plumbing in your apartment is narrow and old, and your toilet is overflowing. As you are desperately plunging, your glasses—the sides of which are wonky from falling asleep in them while reading—slide down the slope of your nose and into the dirty, cresting bowl and you are filled with rage and despair. This feels like a metaphor for something. Not to mention, how the *fuck* can you imagine yourself to be a *first responder* when you respond to an overflowing toilet bowl with such flailing panic and almost-comic ineptitude?

◎

Vermillion, South Dakota, on the Platz. December. Postelection. A candlelight vigil for safety and solidarity. It's cold and snowy and bright. The ceremony concludes with John Lennon's "Imagine" played over the loudspeakers, your neighbors and community members singing along, many of them with tears streaming down their faces. This downtown in a small, rural college town starlit by an immense flickering knot of hope and kindness. When the pictures appear online in the *Vermillion Plain Talk*, someone writes "cucks" in the comment section. No one else in the comments section seems to know what it means. Eventually, someone has to explain that it's an "alt-right" hate slur, shorthand for "cuckolds." Like so many things postelection, it's both disturbingly absurd and absurdly disturbing. The comment is promptly taken down—a tiny flicker of menace against a glittering swathe of goodwill electronically snuffed—but still not without a number of Vermillionaires learning some of the terms within a new-to-them vocabulary of hate.

◎

You want to be a first responder, but it's been difficult, if not downright impossible, for you to write. Part of it has been an issue of focus: the malevolent chaos, the constant unspiraling mess of anxiety-provoking news, the fascistic dictatorial threat of demagoguery, autocracy, kakistocracy. Part of it has been the time spent organizing, disseminating information, signal boosting, signing petitions, sending letters and e-mails, calling and calling and calling on the phone, trying to make your voice *heard* and your opinion *count*, and you're sad and angry and scared all the time, and it's like trying to drink out of a firehose, and it's *exhausting* and, still, it never feels like it's *enough*.

◎

The *spitefulness* of the unraveling.

The unmaking for unmaking's sake.

Like snipping a handmade sweater and tugging and pulling and tugging until all that's left is a snarled tangled mess of yarn. And not that the sweater was perfect. Or that it had been satisfactorily altered to accommodate all sizes, all needs. And, in fact, perhaps the problem is that it was a sweater knitted with stolen yarn with the forced labor of stolen hands. But still. It was painstakingly made. And it provided some warmth, though not enough, and not to everyone.

The *spitefulness* of the unraveling.

The unmaking for unmaking's sake.

Erosion and removal of civil rights for marginalized communities.

Plans to defund women's health care.

Plans to defund the arts and humanities.

The gutting of public schools.

Repeal of regulations to prevent the dumping of toxic waste into streams, contaminating the drinking water, while simultaneously repealing health care access to the very people who'd be the first to get sick.

Dismantling/elimination of the EPA.

Gagging of climate change scientists, erasure of their research.

Repeal of environmental protections and political sanctions, to make big oil bigger.

Plans to develop, mine, drill, and frack in national parks.

Repeal of conflict of interest and anticorruption regulations to benefit the obscenely wealthy.

Going, going, gone . . .

◎

All of it is selfish, and bigoted, and cruel, and stupidly short-sighted, but the one that guts you most viciously is the "modernizing" of the Endangered Species Act to strip away its efficacy in the interests of disaster capitalism.

Going, going, gone . . .

No more whooping cranes. No more condors. No more black-footed ferrets. No more ocelots. No more lynxes. No more gray wolves. No more whales. No more sea otters. No more manatees. No more monarch butterflies. No more honeybees. No more __________.

Going, going, gone . . .

Or the recent House vote to overturn a federal rule barring barbaric wildlife practices: the killing of wolf pups in their dens; the killing of bears and their cubs in hibernation; the use of aircraft to aerially spot, then shoot, grizzly bears; the inhumane use of steel-jawed leghold traps and snares.

Genocide is genocide.

Going, going, gone . . .

◎

Late October, and a poet friend tells you about recent advances in genetics that make de-extinction possible. How there's a biorepository at the Smithsonian's National Museum of Natural History: over 4.2 million cryogenic vials (cryovials) of tissue samples stored in liquid nitrogen or mechanical freezers. How scientists, using DNA collected from remains as a genetic blueprint, can engineer extinct traits into living organisms. Apparently, through splicing woolly mammoth genetic edits into Asian elephant DNA, they are now two years away from creating a "mammophant" hybrid embryo. At the time, you found this wondrous, but also *creepy.* Since the election and inauguration, though, the creepiness factor has greatly abated, now replaced by a manic and desperate *hopefulness.*

◎

You read that the Japanese have recently designed robo-bees that successfully pollinate flowers, using tiny drones, horsehair, and a sticky ion gel. The real bees are disappearing, and scientific research indicates that the two primary culprits are climate change and pesticides that contain neonicotinoids. Without the bees to pollinate their flowers, all vegetables and fruits that require pollination will disappear. What does this mean for a presidential administration that denies climate change? What does this mean for a presidential administration that's so eager to repeal regulations for toxic waste disposal, let alone create new bans against the use of neonicotinoids in pesticides made by corporate giants such as Monsanto?

Everyone seems to feel the robo-bees are disturbing and sinister in a *Black Mirror*–esque kind of way, and yes, you agree, but mostly? You find them to be achingly *sad.*

◎

You used to assume that fish were silent—even though, in a poem once, you fancifully imagined them *singing*—but today you read an article that says fish do, in fact, sing. And that different fish species's calls overlap to form a *chorus*, at dawn and at dusk, like birds singing in the forest. All day long, you play the .MP3 of fish singing in the Australian reefs, and it makes you weep. Because something you thought was silent was instead full of song, and it was filled with song all along. Because now all the things you discover that fill you with wonder, light, and hope are filtered through grief's uneasy shadows of elegy and requiem.

◎

You haven't been able to sleep since the election, and so you stay up late at night, compulsively knitting and crocheting. Hats and scarves and cowls and afghans and an ark of zoological amigurumi and, yes, a pink pussy hat too. It's obviously a self-soothing coping mechanism, but it also feels good to be *making* something. As if, in the midst of all of the unraveling, unmaking, and unspooling, it's an affirmation of *repair*.

A metaphor for the *creative force*, a celebration of *making*.

Artists as the first responders.

Arachne, lace making her world anew.

Philomela, tongue cut out and silenced, looming the story of her rape in woven designs to her sister Procne so that the women can take revenge.

Mothra, spinning her silk cocoon before rising from the environmental wreckage of Monster Island.

The Wind Phone

1.

In your elderly parents' home in Laramie, Wyoming, there is no internet, no Wi-Fi, no cable television (only three channels: one clear, two fuzzy), no cell phone, not even a push-button telephone—only a rotary-dial landline mounted to the kitchen wall, installed when the house was originally built over fifty years ago. It's a strange pinkish beige, with a spiraling curlicue cord that's grubby from use. The bottom of the cracked handset is held together by masking tape and rubber bands.

Everything in this house of clutter, with entire rooms rendered unusable by clinical hoarding, seems to be held together by rubber bands, twine, and old underwear elastics: mail, jars, boxes, pillows. Even the few things that don't require holding together (a large agate paperweight, for example) are garnished with rubber bands. (Why? For just in case? Or perhaps as decoration?) The house itself, with mysterious electrical overloads requiring constant resetting of the circuit breakers, and ominously thumping plumbing, seems a fragile deck of cards rubber banded together against the ubiquitous blasting gales of Wyoming wind.

Your mother sullenly admits that if a call requires the use of a push-button phone tree, your parents just hang up the phone. To dial out requires inserting an index finger into numbered holes, the quick *schwuck* of pullback, then the leisurely glottal rotation of the plastic dialer: an obsolescent sound, the analog rhythm of nostalgia.

2.

On a hilltop garden overlooking Otsuchi, Japan—a century-old town decimated by the 2011 tsunami—a man named Itaru Sasaki has placed a phone booth containing a disconnected rotary-dial phone. Sasaki originally used the phone to speak to a beloved cousin who'd died prior to the tsunami. Sasaki began processing his grief by communicating to his cousin "on the wind." Now people who've lost loved ones in the tsunami come to Otsuchi from all along the Tohoku coast, making pilgrimages to speak to their dead, on the *kaze no denwa*, the "wind phone."

3.

When your Japanese mother calls you on the telephone to tell you that your father has broken his hip, that he's been taken to the hospital in Cheyenne for surgery, she hasn't spoken to you in over three years. The last words she'd said to you were, "You not family anymore. No longer any connection."

You're eight weeks out of cancer surgery and still recovering, but your mother's clearly scared and anxious—alone in the house, unable to drive, unable to write out checks for bills by herself. Even though you'd told your friends that if and when "the call" came you planned on having "good boundaries," you nonetheless find yourself, four days later, driving to Wyoming. You're grateful for your friend Pen, who—having fielded a similar call regarding her father's terminal illness just a few years prior—kindly said, "You don't really know what you'll do when the call comes. No one really knows until it actually comes. But when it comes, you'll know what to do."

Your mother doesn't mention the disowning, or the three years' silence, for which you're uneasily grateful, but there's also something distinctly eerie about it. Has she repressed or rewritten the family history? Has she simply *forgotten*? The severed connection to the past is, frankly, *uncanny*.

4.

There are other lapsed connections as well. The doctors think your father clearly broke his hip due to a fall, even though he doesn't remember falling, and your mother also doesn't remember him taking a fall. Your mother says that for almost two weeks he was in an increasing amount of pain, that he couldn't get out of bed, yet he refused to go to the doctor. One day he was in so much pain he couldn't even speak, and that's when she finally called 911.

Your mother informs you that your father's been having "head trouble" for about two years. But she warns you not to say anything to him about it. She says it will make him angry. When you press her to describe how and when the "head trouble" started, she describes an event that clearly sounds like a stroke. One day your father was in the kitchen, your mother says, and then he suddenly collapsed. He shouted out her name several times. He seemed completely disoriented. She says he couldn't remember where he was or what he was doing. So she put him to bed and gave him an ice pack for his head. Afterward, he had trouble writing his name on checks, she tells you. But then he "got better." The CT scan they do at the hospital before his hip surgery reveals that, indeed, your father did have a stroke at some point in time.

Although he still has occasional periods of lucidity, you're distressed to discover that your father, who used to be a writer and professor, now seems frequently confused. His relationship to language has irrevocably changed. He struggles to find the words for what he wants to convey and ramblingly spirals around a thought with a circular word salad that seems nonsensical until you're eventually able to guess what he's trying to say—finding the objective to his correlative, proffering up the words he's searching for. His physical therapy's complicated by the fact that his body feels, to him, like two parts that don't wish to come together. He mistakes the television remote control for a cell phone, says "eyes" instead of "teeth," "lettuce" instead of "checks."

You don't have the heart to tell your mother that had she been able to identify the "head trouble" as a stroke and called 911, some of these effects might have been reversed. What's possibly more unnerving, however, is that your Japanese mother's English comprehension has obviously deteriorated with age, such that she seems completely unable to detect when your father isn't making sense. Instead, she says that he sounds good, that he's talking "with a strong voice," even when what he's saying is completely jumbled. She rarely understands him, which frustrates him, and he seems utterly confused by what she's trying to communicate to him. You find yourself constantly having to intervene and interpret.

5.

Over ten thousand people have come to Otsuchi to visit the *kaze no denwa* to dial up their dead or missing on the disconnected rotary dial phone. Sometimes they share their daily news or express their regrets. Sometimes they call to say please come back. Sometimes they implore the dead to look out for one another. Sometimes they simply say that they're lonely.

6.

You've been the simultaneous interpreter, the go-between, the bridge, the messenger, interlocutor, long-distance phone line, and scapegoat in your parents' marriage for as long as you can remember.

When you were younger, it was sometimes an occasion of hilarity: both of them stubbornly doubling down in a heated argument with one another, without realizing they were actually in complete agreement, until you were able to detangle the knot of misunderstanding.

Now your mother confuses and agitates your father by talking about the U.S. Bank bill when he's talking about the quarterly tax payment.

Now your father, who apparently doesn't care for his roommate at the Laramie Care Center, has accidentally convinced your mother, by asking for additional clothes to be brought over, that said roommate is *snitching* all of his clothes.

When your father asks your mother if she needs money, your mother interprets this as your father expressing anxiety about their finances. She insists on interpreting this as a request that she squirrel away all of her cash to pay for his medical bills because they have no other money. Whereas your father's simply trying to make sure your mother has enough cash on hand to use as needed while he's convalescing.

Repeatedly, you are called to the phone to attempt to translate their miscommunications.

Repeatedly, they take turns raising (occasionally very legitimate) complaints against one another with you.

Repeatedly, they expect you to take sides.

Repeatedly, it occurs to you that your mother's emotionally and physically violent borderline rages and your father's less-frequent-but-nonetheless-brutal bursts of anger may have been, at least in part, about projecting unspoken resentments toward one another onto you.

Tellingly, your mother unloads on you right as you're about to make your departure, after three weeks of depending on you for nonstop assistance. She castigates your father, then tells you that you're his daughter, that you're just like him. No, she decides.

You're even *worse* than your father. She tells you a litany of the ways in which you're a horrible person: that you're lazy because you "didn't want to come out" and she spent over twenty-four hours in childbirth; that once, when you were sixteen, you told her to stop bothering you when she burst into the bathroom uninvited, sniffing you to see if she could detect the smell of sex after you'd returned from a date; that you're "a complete selfish." You've been steeling yourself for an outburst like this for the entire three weeks you've been in Wyoming, but you won't lie, it still hurts.

7.

In the most heartbreaking phone calls made on the *kaze no denwa*, the callers apologize for not having been able to save their dead.

8.

Later, when you call your mother from the road—fully prepared to tell her that she'd been verbally abusive to you and it wasn't okay, fully prepared to be disowned again (the typical pattern of your interactions)—she grudgingly mutters, "Sorry."

It's the first time in your life you've ever heard your mother apologize. A part of you realizes your mother's done the mental math and knows that she *needs* you to pay the bills, coordinate with doctors' offices, make arrangements for ride services, renew prescriptions, and set up grocery deliveries. That she *needs* you to purchase a walker, set up occupational and physical therapy services, and negotiate with contractors to make the required accessibility accommodations to the house in order for your father to be released from nursing home rehab at the end of the summer. Nonetheless, you accept her apology.

You wonder if your mother's memory issues—as disturbing as they are to witness—have possibly softened some of the effects of her mental illness. While you notice that she mostly keeps initiating and repeating the same familiar conversations of grievance, she occasionally shares memories of her life in Japan—a life you'd always asked about when you were growing up, only to be told, "Don't stick nose in my business!" Now she sometimes likes to speak of her girlhood friends: Kinu, who was a show-off; Suzi, the mischievous rascal; Kiyoe, the quiet one; or her older sister, Kazue, who was always late and who always did exactly as she pleased. "All dead now," she says, sadly. Some of their deaths she learned about from friends and relatives. Some of their deaths were only presumed when the phone calls to America stopped coming.

Sometimes, uncannily, she speaks of you in the third person. "Lee Ann used to do this." Or "Lee Ann used to do that." And occasionally, she seems to forget who you are altogether, addressing you as if you were a new acquaintance at a tea party, asking polite questions such as, "Do you have husband?"

9.

Your father announces that he doesn't want to be visited in the Laramie Care Center, so although you're in town for three weeks, you and your mother only go to see him twice. The second time you visit, he hands you a large bundle of used, food-smudged dinner napkins. He's apparently been hoarding them inside his hoody. He insists on giving them to you, and not your mother. He orders you to put them in a plastic bag, keep them someplace safe. He tells you they are the bills documenting his expenses.

When you express your concern about this to your mother, she tells you that your father's sad that you're leaving. That he wants to give something to you.

"But they're mostly used napkins," you say.

"That's because he doesn't want us to have to pay for expensive napkin," she replies, all smiles. "We save money! Don't have to buy!"

And because your mother seems happy, you leave it at that.

Perhaps, as in any game of telephone, when the transmission becomes garbled, maybe it's enough that the people on either end are, at least temporarily, at peace.

Anhedonia in the Anthropocene

1. SUX → ORD → ANH

The airplane tilts and honeycombed squares of light slide down the opposite wall, dripping into the seat rests and tray tables. The sweetness fades. Like a frozen smile meant to reassure, that quickly falters into a slippery grimace.

You used to love to travel: the jostled shiny hustle of airports, skid of roller bag wheels skimming the ubiquity of flecked tile, a cacophonous assembly, merge and remerge. Like the annual staging of the sandhill cranes gathering on the sand bars of the Platte during spring migration—before flying off, family groups reassembled, business completed, to distant locales.

You used to love the mysterious promise of the three-letter airport codes: OMA → ATL → PDX, SUX → ORD → LGA, FSD → MSP → SLC → ANC → HOM.

Lately, maybe because you do it so often, it's become something that you mostly *endure*. A fourteen-hour obstacle course beginning with a middle-of-the-night drive from your small town to the airport to arrive in time for the morning leg of your flight—followed by X-rays, pat-downs, the parsing of 3.4-ounce fluids into clear containers, inevitable delays unraveling into missed flights. A gauntlet you try to survive while hungry, cranky, and tired.

The time you used to spend daydreaming from the window seat aloft in the froth of nozzled wads of clouds now spent in the more convenient aisle seat, distracting yourself with a book or game. Everyone insists on keeping the shades pulled down anyways. You're not sure why.

More and more, you think of Elizabeth Bishop's "Questions of Travel": "Continent, city, country, society: / the choice is never wide and never free. / And here, or there . . . No. Should we have stayed at home, / wherever that may be?"

2. Open the Pod Bay Doors, Hal

Anhedonia is such a beautiful word. It sounds like some magical, Latinate destination. Like Caledonia, except sunny. Or a planet from another galaxy—one wreathed in a crown of cold bright moons and lush with carnivorous plants, strangling tendrils of melancholic vines.

But the reality of Anhedonia as destination is far less glamorous.

It's the sinking ship bristling with rats, all the life preservers tossed out days ago like candies at a parade.

The name of the pawn shop where all the shiny things have been hocked.

Epithet for the drained-out phone battery that refuses to hold a charge.

A euphemism for the cruel silver of the melon baller as it scoops out sweet flesh all the way down to the thin nubbly rind.

Synonym for the empty fortune cookie.

3. Matryoshkas on Monster Island

The seed of tumor in the malignant fruit of your womb excised by a robot, your dissected lymph nodes miraculously clean, it seems, and you know you are ridiculously lucky. You know you should be happy, happy, happy!

But instead, you feel like a thrift-shop Russian nesting doll, a hollowed-out Matryoshka, missing the two smallest dolls.

As far as cancer goes, you've rolled boxcars in craps—no chemo, no radiation—and you have a five-year survival rate of 88 percent. Although the statistics are bleak in the event of recurrence, the numbers, as they say, look *good*.

You *should* be grateful: for the good outcome, for your employment and your health insurance, for your friends who listened to you crying on the phone, who drove you to the hospital, who sat with you, who picked you up and took you home, who lined up rows of easy-to-reach soups on your kitchen counter. And while you're practically *shoulding* all over yourself, the darker and deeper truth is that while yes, you're intellectually aware of the numerous reasons you have for gratitude, you still feel depression's flatline relentlessly clouding the monitor of your emotional life to dull static.

As an abuse survivor, hypervigilance is your shadow self, your twin sibling, your alter ego, your superpower, your Kryptonite. You imagine Mothra as your avatar, the exquisite awfulness of sensing minute shifts in your surroundings through the delicate feathery fronds of your antennae. How you easily scan and read people for potential danger, how you often know things about them in advance (but pretend that you don't know these things unless and until they trust you enough to tell you), how easily fried you become from sifting through the electricity of their complex emotional weather.

But your antennae are useless when it comes to sensing the dangers ticking away within your own body. Still, you obsessively scan anyways—following the adrenaline loop-de-loop of fear coursing from this twinge, that ache, this crashing fatigue, this chronic pain—like a PET scan following the blossomed imagery of radioactive tracers.

4. Pink Flamingos

You monitor the new and unrelenting chronic pain in your lower spine and hips like an absurdly surreal ornithological specimen that has settled into your backyard. You scrutinize it with binoculars, track its movement throughout the day. You tiptoe around it, careful not to startle it. You adjust your day around its activities.

You throw blue pellets of naproxen at it, spritz it with minty liniments.

All of this becomes a dance, with plumage, that you perform. A fandango of feint and parry, rising vertiginous spirals of red-spasmed veronicas, a welder's torch spray of electric castanets igniting a neuronal pathway of hot flinty sparks.

When it fades back into camouflage, you feel unschackled, unshadowed.

A bitter lozenge trickles down the back of your throat, the hard frost of pain evaporates, and finally, you feel as if you can think your thoughts again.

5. Salt and the Open Wound

Your metaphor for vulnerability is to be like a mollusk without a shell—that feeling of moist tenderness exposed to the elements, like something pulled inside out, of coming unshelled/unhoused/undone, of feeling like a raw morsel scenting the air, waiting for predators to come.

Once, in Oysterville, Washington, you had a meeting of the minds with a giant Pacific banana slug. A cool, luna-moth green—chilly and sticky as a peeled kiwi—with inquisitive antennae that it could shyly retract back down under its mantle. You felt as if you had befriended an alien.

It was weighty and dense as melon flesh, like a binding spell cast on water, and moved with the fluidity of a shimmering ink rollerball. You regarded each other with curiosity for many minutes, and then, before it dried out or took in too much salt from your hands, you placed it back outside in the rain again.

Thinking of the deliberate cruelty of pouring salt on a slug makes you feel *stricken*. Although they do not have pain receptors in the human sense, it's a physiologically similar effect to getting salt in your eye. Through the process of osmosis (when a solution meets a permeable membrane), the slug flushes water through its membranes to attempt to dilute the saltwater solution formed by the intrusion of salt in its mucous, and it dehydrates itself.

On the planet of Anhedonia, you feel like a slug under assault by the daily news—white crystals shaking and shaking down from the sky. Salt in an open wound.

6. Merry Christmas, Baby

One week before Thanksgiving and the Keystone Pipeline spills 210,000 gallons, contaminating soil near the Lake Traverse Reservation and raising concerns about bitumen leaking into and contaminating the Crow Creek drainage ditch—a small tributary to the James River, which is a major water supplier for the state of South Dakota.

Although you try to keep your eyes wide open, to remain attentive, to witness, to not check out and shut down in the midst of the rising tide of ecocide, gun violence, institutionally sanctioned racism, murderous tax and health care bills, and the terrible but unsurprising (at least not to you) chorus of *#metoo, #metoo, #metoo* (because of course, yes, *#youtoo, #youtoo, #youtoo*), there's a viral video that you nonetheless cannot bear to watch. And yet you watch it anyways, again and again and again.

In this video, taken by photographers and biologists Paul Nicklen and Cristina Mittermeier, an emaciated polar bear staggers on dry land and rummages through empty trash cans seasonally used by Inuit fishers on Baffin Island, in the Canadian territory of Nunavut. Coming up empty, the polar bear simply collapses.

It is illegal to feed polar bears in Canada, and even if it were legal, they require hundreds of pounds of seal meat per meal. Miles away from the nearest village, and not in possession of a tranquilizer gun, there was nothing the photographers could do but document the miserable scene. Polar bear scientist Ian Stirling says that if global warming continues, "the Arctic marine ecosystem as we know it will no longer exist."

Contrast this with the ubiquitous Coca-Cola Christmas ads in which plump and fluffy polar bears cavort on ice floes with polar bear cubs and penguins, swilling bottles of Coke over a soundtrack of the Beach Boys singing "Merry Christmas, Baby," and basically? It makes you want to slit your wrists.

All of this triangulates with the constant anxiety over your snowbound elderly parents in Laramie, Wyoming, who have turned away all of their home health care services, who refuse to answer their door when the social worker comes to do a welfare check. Your father is losing weight. Your father is driving the car, even though he isn't supposed to. Your father isn't using the shower assist and has fallen, possibly reinjuring his broken hip. They've rescinded permission for their doctors to communicate with you about their medical status. Your mother says your father has "leg trouble" again, that he's unable to get out of bed to go to the bathroom. "Don't tell anyone," she whispers into the phone. You call their doctor's office. The doctor says they've missed several appointments and that when the nurses try to call, your parents refuse to answer the phone. You put in a request for another welfare check. Your parents refuse to let the social worker into the house. You don't know what to do, aside from documenting this miserable scene.

7. Winter of Our Discontent

Driving I-25 in New Mexico past the Pecos National Forest during the summer, you were startled by a bear on the highway. A large brown bear. Lying down in the middle of the highway. It seemed to be sleeping. A large brown bear sleeping in the middle of the highway.

Until you realized that it wasn't sleeping. It was roadkill.

The not-sleeping bear haunted you for the rest of your drive to Laramie. It began to feel like a portent of sorts. A metaphor for your hollowed-out core, the shrinking polar ice caps, your elderly parents' evaporating memory.

Earlier that summer, when you dug out family photos and looked at them with your mother, you realized she frequently didn't recognize herself. "Who this?" she'd demand. "That's you," you'd tell her. At first, she wouldn't believe you, before finally exclaiming "Good grief!" in exasperation.

You worked all the way down to the wire of the fall semester's start that summer, frantically preparing your parents' house for your father's return from the nursing home where he'd been rehabbing his broken hip. It was an intense whirlwind of cleaning, organizing, clearing pathways, ordering adaptive equipment, and hiring contractors to make accessibility renovations. Every day, your father would impatiently ask if he could come home yet, and every day, you'd have to remind him that the earliest date the contractors could finish work on the house would be early September. Oftentimes, he'd become agitated and angry, blaming you for his cognitive impairments, accusing you of sinister collaborations with his medical health care providers: "If you had half a brain, you'd know you're endangering me!" he'd yell. "Why can't you learn to keep your big fat mouth shut?"

What happens in the moment when you realize that a sleeping bear isn't really sleeping?

The tangled vines of melancholia on the planet of Anhedonia, they flourish, invade, and scourge. Like black mold. Like gray matter on the brain. Like cancer metastasizing.

The days darken, and light snow occasionally shakes down from the sky in a crisp, crystalline salt.

The days darken. Like a window being blacked out, the aperture of light gets shorter and smaller.

Homeward Bound

1.

Sunset around Cheyenne, and you are descending from the Abraham Lincoln Memorial Monument at the summit of I-80, spiraling downward in the dark toward Laramie. It is spring break, and you have seven days to move your parents from their house, where they have lived for over fifty years, into assisted living. The tenth hour of driving, and as you circle down the switchbacks, you have the sensation that your consciousness is about to float out and away from your body. The drive is two hours longer than is comfortable for you to complete in one day, but there's a limited window of time, so you press forward. When you coast down into the foothills, and the lights of Laramie finally come sparkling into view—a multifaceted glister, the "gem city of the plains"—you are exhausted and relieved.

2.

Although you've spent the entire prior week making daily encouragements on the phone to your mother to come up with a list of things she absolutely wants to take with her to the new apartment, you come home to find that she is drowning in minutiae.

The house is an overflowing cornucopia of hoarding, and your mother is unable to prioritize. Instead, she's bogged down in what she's willing to "give up." Mostly, she obsesses over her clothing. She's made a small stack of clothes, largely bought from garage sales, that she's decided she's willing to donate to Goodwill, but she keeps going through the stacks, again and again, trying on the clothes, and changing her mind. She agonizes over sacks of garage sale costume jewelry, trying on plastic necklace after plastic necklace—occasionally reluctantly setting aside a piece or two to discard.

3.

Your mother "hides" things in the middle of the night, so that people won't be able to come into the house and *snitch* them. While this level of intense paranoia is distressingly familiar from your childhood, the items that your mother deems legitimately *snitchable* has become radically misplaced. She hides the garbage bags because someone might break into the house and *snitch* her nice garbage bags. She hides the handbags she was setting aside to donate to Goodwill because someone might break into the house and *snitch* her nice handbags. She hides the Ramen noodles because someone might break into the house and *snitch* her nice Ramen noodles. In the meantime, you make regular sweeps of the house to take custody of social security cards, drivers' licenses, checkbooks, credit cards, and cash—lying around in the open, mixed in with junk—to set them aside for safekeeping.

In a self-fulfilling prophecy, when she can't remember that she's hidden her stash of *snitchable* items the following day, she becomes convinced that someone has broken into the house and *snitched* her nice trash bags, her nice handbags, her nice Ramen noodles. If, several days later, she discovers these items crammed into some bizarre location, she angrily accuses you of putting her stuff in strange places where she can't find it.

In a more charming incarnation of this phenomenon, you discovered the summer before that your mother had taken to hiding chocolate from your father. But since she forgets where she's hidden it, she leaves notes for herself on the refrigerator in Japanese, which your father can't read.

4.

In the meantime, you make a litany of phone calls, fill out reams of paperwork, forward the mail, purchase a new mattress for your parents, buy numerous boxes and bins, and pack up necessities. Several days before the actual move is scheduled, you tell your mother that a decision needs to be made regarding the furniture she wants to take with her.

You list off a reasonable number of furniture items for the space of the apartment, then ask if your mother's sure that she wants to bring the sofa—the one piece of furniture she seems irrevocably committed to. You wonder if your mother would be happier with, for example, another buffet cabinet, where she can display more of her china collection, or her beloved Japanese dolls.

Your mother becomes furious, says that you are always "against her" and "never on her side." The sofa springs have been completely shot for well over a decade. You point out that the sofa will take up a lot of room in the apartment for a piece that no one can actually *sit* in.

"Sofa not for sitting," says your mother.

"What is it for then?" you ask.

"For show *off*," she replies, as if you're incredibly stupid.

5.

Despite the impossible amount of work that needs to be done, and even though you've been doing most of the cooking, your mother insists on making pineapple chicken, one of your father's favorites, the day before the move. She says the chicken needs to be used, but you wonder if some part of her is aware, as you are aware, that this is probably the last meal that she will ever cook.

It is delicious.

Taped to the grimy kitchen cupboard next to the stove is a notecard, in your father's quavery handwriting. It reads:

Dear Yoshiko,
Don't forget to turn off the stove.
Love, Robert

6.

The morning the movers are scheduled to arrive, you wake up with an overwhelming sense of desolation. The Wyoming wind is stirring up the crows in the backyard pines into a raucous cacophony. Your mother, who you discover curled up, catlike, on your feet at the bottom of your bed in the basement, says it is the sound of *death*.

The movers are quick, strong, and amazingly competent. Nonetheless, your mother—made anxious by strangers in her house, touching her things—hovers around them, attempting to micromanage, attempting to help.

You're finally able to get her settled in a chair, out of their way. When the movers lift up the sofa of contention to reveal a shotgun stashed behind it, your mother giggles. "Oh, that's your *father*!" she says, as if to imply what a *card* he is, as if the movers had uncovered some sort of eccentrically hilarious, vintage salt-and-pepper shaker collection. Earlier in the week, you'd canvassed the nightstand and dresser drawers for handguns, but this, you hadn't anticipated.

7.

When your father's transported to the new apartment from the Laramie Care Center, where he's been rehabbing for the past three months after another fall, you're shocked to see how much he's visibly deteriorated. His hands shake to the point that it's difficult for him to feed himself. Occasionally, one hand floats up to the side of his face. There's something strangely lovely about this gesture—fingers quavering softly like underwater sea anemone. When he notices his raised left hand fluttering by the side of his face, like something escaped, he captures it with his right hand, brings it back down to his lap.

Your mother watches you watching your father. When she catches your glance, she puffs out her cheeks, crosses her eyes, then exaggeratedly waves her hand by the side of her face. You're horrified to realize that your mother is *mocking* your father. When your father follows your gaze back over to your mother, she quickly drops her hand into her lap, makes a faux-innocent, *ajapa* face.

Early in the afternoon, during the cognitive assessment test, your mother charms the nurse into giving her clues for the correct answers. She claims she doesn't understand English very well, that *no one* can remember three random objects.

"I'm eighty-something!" she exclaims. "When I go downstairs to get something from basement, I completely forget what I go down there for!" Later, she brags, "I get A+!" even though she thinks it's 2017 instead of 2018, that the month is April instead of March, and her drawing of a clock is somewhat Dali-esque.

Your father, on the other hand, insists that the year is 1972 and that he lives in the state of New Mexico. He can't remember the name of the city he lives in. Behind the nurse's back, your mother makes a series of indecipherable hand signals to your father, mouths out answers, which are—hilariously, even though this probably shouldn't be funny—*wrong*. You realize she's trying to help your father *cheat* on his cognitive assessment test. When he responds with his own wrong answer, she rolls her eyes in disgust.

Later that afternoon, your mother has a mood crash. "Why I have to live such horrible life?" she asks. "I wish I never leave Japan. Nobody here can help me. I wish your father's father or your father's brother still alive. They can take care of us."

You tell her that *you* are here, that you will help her, that you promise to take care of her. "How you can help?" she asks. "You not a man. You just a *girl*!"

After dinner, though, she keeps talking about how your father's former mentor, Dr. Ruth Hudson, always used to say your father had beautiful hands. And you wonder if there was a part of your mother that had seen it earlier too—the weirdly ethereal beauty of your father's hand, sparked by the electricity of misfiring neurons, fluttering unbidden at the side of his face, with a strange kind of grace.

8.

The night before you drive back to South Dakota, you stay up late and do your best to close down your parents' house until you're able to return in the summer. You take out the trash, unplug appliances, clear out perishables from the refrigerator, locate and pack up any valuables and sensitive information. The house seems uncanny, damaged—piles and piles of stuff upon stuff everywhere, with strange abscesses of emptiness where furniture was removed, like wounds.

While rescuing checkbooks from handbags, mixed in with other handbags slated for possible donation to Goodwill, you find a bag filled with an *obscene* amount of cash. It's impossible for you to tell if your mother has hidden, and then forgotten, this *mob-boss-going-on-the-lam* amount of cash or if this is her idea of *safekeeping*—her solution for safely storing her expensive jewelry apparently being to hide it in the bedroom in a plastic bag filled with rags to "fool the robbers" into thinking it was garbage.

The next day is Sunday, the banks are closed, and even if they weren't, the guardianship papers aren't finalized yet, which means you don't have access to make deposits to your parents' bank accounts. So you count the cash, take a photograph of it, then email your parents' probate attorney to officially declare the cash as part of your parents' estate, and to document that you've taken custody of the bag for safekeeping. It seems both ludicrous and surreal that you're going to have to drive across state lines with a panic-attack-inducing, *drug dealer* amount of cash. You disguise it in a trash bag—perhaps you are your mother's daughter, after all?—and stash it on the floor underneath a pillow behind the driver's seat.

All day long, eastward on I-80, blackbirds houndstooth the leftover scrum of snow, stipple the roiling sloughs. Your entire body hurts from packing and unpacking and you've barely gotten any sleep all week. You're hallucination-level tired. Somewhere just north of Omaha, you feel yourself leaving your body—floating off into the darkness to simply disappear. It occurs to you that you have no business operating a motor vehicle. You pull over at the nearest rest area, attempt to quell the rising panic. Shortly after merging back onto I-29, you feel yourself leaving your body once again. Now you're having a full-fledged panic attack, and you inch down the highway. Every time you feel yourself floating out of your body into the darkness, you pull over to the side with your hazards on and try to talk yourself down.

When the golden Super 8 sign materializes on the horizon outside of Onawa, Iowa, it seems like nothing short of a miracle. Even though home's less than an hour and a half away, you pull in, park, unpack your luggage and the trash bag in which you've hidden your mother's Gollum hoard of cash, and check in. Above the front desk, there's a sign for a whirlpool suite. You say that you'll take it. You buy yourself a candy bar too. And in the Super 8, you melt like chocolate into the hot wet where, buffeted by the jets, you cry and cry and cry.

Five Loaded Handguns

> One must never place a loaded rifle on the stage if it isn't going to go off. It's wrong to make promises you don't mean to keep.—ANTON CHEKHOV

Handgun #1:

You find the first loaded handgun when your knee brushes up against something hard—protruding slightly from underneath the mattress of your childhood bed. You pull out the triangular, wedge-shaped case, unzip it to find a revolver inside. You're shocked to discover that it's fully loaded. It's not just the shock of it, you're also kind of pissed. It's a single-action revolver and doesn't have a hammer block to keep it from accidentally cocking, which means it isn't drop proof.

You use your thumb to release the cylinder latch and swing out the cylinder, then push down on the ejector rod to release the first cartridge. You rotate the cylinder and repeat five more times, then double-check to make sure all six chambers are empty before swinging the cylinder back into place and zipping the revolver into its case again.

Prior to moving your parents into the assisted living center, you'd cleared out the nightstand next to their bed, in part to make sure your American grandfather's pistol wasn't still hidden there. You didn't want any guns accidentally being transported in the move. You'd been relieved to find the drawers were only filled with junk: grimy rubber bands, empty aspirin bottles, dead batteries, broken flashlights, and burned-down candle nubs. When the movers came, though, and lifted up the sofa, there was a double-barrel shotgun hidden behind it, which you stashed in your parents' bedroom closet.

After finding the loaded handgun, you pull the shotgun back out of the closet, unzip the leather case, and thumb the break-open switch until the shotgun hinges open. You're disturbed to find that the shotgun, too, is loaded. You remove the shells, double-check the chambers, and reverse the hinge action until the shotgun closes with a click.

It's not that you didn't know there were guns in the house. Your father used to be an avid hunter after all—a sport he enjoyed with your American grandfather and uncle. You grew up with guns and were taught how to handle them at an early age, although now, as an adult, you definitively prefer *not* to. What troubles you is that the guns are *loaded*, so very much *at the ready*—clearly not intended for hunting antelope or sage grouse but rather to protect the house from possible intruders. What troubles you is the way they grossly violate everything you know, everything you'd been taught by your father, about gun safety etiquette.

Handgun #2:

Your father has made of your old bedroom a hamster's nest of hoarding: old bills dating back to the 1970s mixed in with junk mail mixed in with sensitive financial and legal documents mixed in with cracked eight-track tapes mixed in with books mixed in with gun magazines mixed in with papers mixed in with empty prescription bottles mixed in with stale chocolate mixed in with used urinary pads mixed in with discount-bin video cassette tapes mixed in with pamphlets for injectable erectile dysfunction meds—all stuffed into precariously stacked and collapsing cardboard flats of Ramen noodle containers. You find the second loaded handgun sandwiched between two of these cardboard flats.

You're spending an entire month of your summer sleeping on your parents' living room floor, despite your debilitating spinal stenosis, working on securing and decluttering your parents' house. You consider bringing up the presence of the loaded handguns with your parents when you go to see them at the assisted living center, but after dinner, they begin fighting about the Fat Juice, which is what your Japanese mother calls the vanilla Ensure they both like. Back in their apartment after dinner, your father suggests that everyone have a cold drink, which is his way of saying that he wants a Fat Juice.

"No!" your mother tells him. "You drinking my Fat Juice like *water*! So *expensive*! And then you going to go to bathroom on new mattress your daughter *bought* for us."

"It's the only kind of cold drink that's any *good*," your father says.

"Let him have a Fat Juice," you say, since you've been bankrolling the Fat Juice supply. "I'm happy to buy you both as much Fat Juice as you want."

"You shut up," your mother says to you. "Don't try stick your nose in our business." She opens the refrigerator and offers a half-empty, flat diet ginger ale to your father. "Here, you finish this first," she says.

"I don't *like* that!" your father yells.

"Then you don't get a cold drink!" your mother yells back.

"*Good!*" your father yells. He rolls his wheelchair into the bedroom and stares out the window.

"Your father, he drinking up all my Fat Juice," your mother says to you, sotto voce. "And then last night, do you know what happen? I been waiting all day to drink my Fat Juice and he drinking *glub*

glub glub three or four. But I been saving mine until end of day to enjoy, and then I ask him if he want half, and you know what he say?"

"What did he say?" I ask.

"He say no, he don't *want* any," she says. "What kind of *person* going to act that way?" she asks.

Handgun #3:

The third loaded handgun shows up tucked into the handrail of your childhood bed up next to the white desk where you used to do your homework. You recognize this handgun as your American grandfather's service revolver, an old Colt, from World War I. Your grandfather, who was born in 1899, lied about his age and enlisted at the tail end of the war, against his mother's wishes.

You wait until after dinner at the assisted living center to find a moment alone with your mother to ask her what's going on with all of the loaded handguns in the house. When you tell her you've found three so far, she cheerfully says, "Oh, we *need* those to *shoot* people when they going to try and break in our house and *snitch* our money! Because they going to try and cut open screen *window* and snitch everything! Poor daddy, they already snitch his Jeep tires when his car was in the driveway and we have to sell his car. But you know what? He buy that car without ask me and he *snitch* my money to buy it. If I know so many gun there, I going to shoot your father when he being *tonkachi* head!"

Handgun #4:

The fourth loaded handgun is a small Ruger revolver, still housed in its original cardboard packaging. It's tightly wedged under your bed along with stacks of old phonebooks and back issues of the *American Rifleman*, *Guns and Ammo*, and *Combat Handguns*.

You find the handgun shortly before discovering a #11 envelope in a raft of paperwork next to your father's manual typewriter on your old white desk. "Mike McCarty File" is typewritten on the front of the file. Mike McCarty is the name of the boy who lived across the street and molested you when you were nine years old.

There's a small slip of lined notebook paper, that reads, in your father's handwriting:

About 4:45–5 on bicycle.
West on Hillside to LaPrele, W. on rt. Side to Corthell.
Boy began following on last part of LaPrele.
Crossed to Corthell.
Boy stopped her and wouldn't let pass in front of 204 Corthell.
Hand in jacket pocket.
Said he had gun and would shoot if she tried to get away.
Forced her to front porch behind screen.

The notes neglect to say what happened to you behind the front porch screen. The notes also decline to name Mike McCarty. Afterward, your parents told you that you'd been stupid, that you should have asked to see the gun. At one point you remember your father saying to you, with impatience and disgust, that you should have been able to properly identify a *real* handgun.

There's an invoice from the psychiatrist, who'd been referred by Mike McCarty's father. Dr. McCarty adamantly denied that his son had committed the molestation, even though you'd identified Mike McCarty down to very particular, minute details. The psychiatrist, who was a colleague of Dr. McCarty's, said you were mistaken in your identification of Mike McCarty.

Your parents declined to press charges, saying that it would be "too expensive," that Dr. McCarty was a "rich doctor," and that it might be "traumatizing" for you to have to say what happened in court.

In the envelope, there are also a series of newspaper clippings from the *Laramie Daily Boomerang*—mostly district court notices and sheriff's calls involving Mike McCarty. Two years after the incident, there's a short article about a lawsuit in the amount of $1.5 million filed by Dr. McCarty against Blue Cross and Blue Shield for allegedly refusing to pay insurance claims to cover Mike McCarty's hospitalization at the Meninger Clinic for "an emotional disorder." Three years after the article about the lawsuit, there's a police report stating that Mike McCarty was arrested for armed robbery at a Foster's Country Store (court notices in the envelope indicate that he was found guilty and sentenced a year later), during which he fired a small handgun in the air before taking all of the money from the cash register and fleeing on foot.

You don't necessarily know what to make or think of the Mike McCarty File. A sense that perhaps your father was profoundly troubled by what had happened? Schadenfreude? That your father wished to see justice done, as long as it was administered by someone else or for something else? You wonder how many other girls were molested before Mike McCarty's parents hospitalized him at the Meninger Clinic for his "emotional disorder."

Later that night, you slip on one of the narrow "goat trails"—perilously strewn with several layers of papers, magazines, and garbage—you'd been using to navigate your way in and out of the room. As you fall, knocking into a Jenga-esqe stack of cardboard Ramen flats filled with papers and junk, there's an immediate domino effect and wobbly towers of books and magazines, and more precarious stacks of filled cardboard Ramen flats come tumbling down in an avalanche. It takes you a full half hour to unblock the door so that you can leave the room again.

Handgun #5:

The fifth loaded handgun is disguised in a grey wool Argyle sock with teal diamonds and red accent stitching. You pull it out from underneath a sheaf of papers and magazines as you near the lower strata of cardboard Ramen flats on the bed. The argyle sock holster is so absurd it makes you laugh, and you keep turning around corny jokes in your mind of the "Is that a loaded handgun in your sock or are you just unhappy to see me?" variety.

In the meantime, you've been telling your friends, who call to see how things are going, that you've renamed yourself Fawn Hall, as you've spent entire days at a time shredding sensitive documents in order to protect your parents from identity theft. The first shredder—one that you found in your parents' living room, but which they apparently never used—breaks after less than half an hour of use. So you head to the local Walmart and purchase the largest shredder that you can carry. Never in your life had you considered a document shredder a sexy purchase, but this shredder? It can shred fourteen sheets at a time, including credit cards, for a full continuous half hour! Eventually, you get a system going in which you Netflix Downton Abbey at the dining room table, using your iPhone as a hot spot, while feeding the shredder, which you've placed on a vintage yellow metal Stylaire step stool chair, with your left hand.

When you call your parents to let them know you won't be coming for dinner at the assisted living center because you want to make sure you finish your work on the house before the month is over, your father asks you what work you're doing at the house. You tell him, as you'd informed him numerous times earlier, that you're clearing the house of sensitive documents and shredding any unnecessary papers that contain personal information to protect them from identity theft.

"No!" your father yells at you, then hangs up the phone.

Several minutes later, your mother calls back to tell you not to shred any more documents. In fact, she tells you not to throw away, shred, or even *touch* anything in the house.

"But that's the reason I'm here," you tell her. "Remember? We talked about it so many times. I'm here to secure the house and clear it out so that it's ready to sell, in case that's something you want to do down the line."

"We let you be guest and stay in our nice house so you have to *obey*! Don't touch *anything*!" your mother yells into the phone. "Promise me! If you don't promise it means you don't care *anything* about your father and me. *Promise*!"

So you promise, even as you know that as soon as you are off the phone, because you are your father's guardian and conservator, you will resume shredding documents. Because everything is always/already fraught. This is the gauntlet of loaded guns that you must disarm.

Shortly after FawnHallGate, your mother decides she wants to see the house. When you take her there, she manically packs up an impossible hodgepodge of belongings to bring back to the assisted living center. You tell her it's going to make her space too crowded, but she insists, so you load up the car and, with your damaged spine on fire, move everything into your parents' apartment. Later that evening, she asks if you've seen a black bag full of money at the house. You explain that it isn't safe to leave that much cash unattended in a house that sits empty for months at a time. You let her know that you've put the cash into a safe deposit box for safekeeping. You tell her the cash has been declared to your parents' probate lawyer and volunteer to show her the Listing of Assets filed with the court. At the time, she just says, "Oh. Okay."

Two weeks later, you'll be at an artist's residency, and when you make your daily phone call to check on your parents, your mother will shout, "How *dare* you! *Shame* on you! Snitcher! Liar! Thief!" before hanging up on you. She's decided that she's furious with you. She says the only way you can make things right with her is to immediately take the cash out of the safety deposit box and send it to her in the mail so she can keep it underneath her bed at the assisted living center. When you tell her you can't do that, she becomes enraged.

"You such complete stink! You such complete horrible!" your mother yells at you over the phone. "You not my daughter anymore!"

And there it is, the loaded gun.

The one that always goes off like a shotgun blast to your face.

Leftovers

1. Vigil

The call comes late in the afternoon, New Year's Day. Your father's fallen in his apartment in the assisted living center. He's not responsive, and he's been taken to the hospital by ambulance. When the hospital finally follows up with you, the news is not good. Your father struck his head in the fall and has a large brain bleed. As his legal guardian, it's now up to you to make the difficult decisions.

The doctor tells you that, one way or another, the brain bleed will ultimately be the cause of your father's death. You ask the doctor what your father's prognosis would be with the same size of brain bleed if he were a young man in good physical condition, without his numerous health issues. The doctor says, "Not good."

So you tell them not to intubate. You tell them to make your father as comfortable as possible.

When you call your mother, who left Japan sixty-four years ago to elope with your father, she's already fuming. "Such stupid!" she says. "He so crazy! I tell him to use nice walker you buy for him, but he don't want to use. Then *bonk*! He fall down."

You tell your mother your father doesn't have long, that you've made arrangements for the assisted living center to drive her to the hospital in the morning so she can sit with him. And then, unable to sleep, you sit up and fret. At 2:00 in the morning, the hospital calls to notify you that your father has quietly passed.

2. Such Stink

On the second day of driving, you arrive in time to have dinner with your mother at the assisted living center. Afterward, you return to her apartment. Once inside the door, she vigorously motions you inside her bedroom, shuts the bedroom door, then whispers that she has something to tell you.

"Your father, he such *stink*!" she says. "He *snitch* all my money, and then you know what?"

"What?" you ask, dumbfounded.

"He give away all my money to his *girlfriend*! But first he take several of his girlfriends out to lunch at nice restaurant downtown! Over sixty years marry, and he *never* take me to nice restaurant downtown!"

When you gently try to explain the wild *unlikelihood* of your frail, wheelchair-using father *snitching* all of her money and *Lothario-ing* it up at the assisted living center, your mother becomes agitated and angry. You recognize so clearly the elaborate, paranoid, painfully disruptive, and intricately illogical conspiracies that held your house emotionally hostage throughout your childhood, now magnified by dementia. You decide that—no matter how much your mother's misconceptions pain you, no matter how *whack-a-doodle* they may be—given that she's lost her husband of sixty-four years, your job will be to hold space for her and to give her, barring serious illegality, *whatever* she wants or needs.

So instead of trying to talk your mother out of the notion that your father snitched her money and gave it all away to his new girlfriend, you simply listen and sympathize. When she asks, "What's *matter* with him? Why he *do* such stink thing to me?" you remind her that he was suffering from dementia (which your mother likes to refer to as "head trouble"). Your mother says, "That's right. He kuru-kuru-pa." She circles her index finger around her ear. "All the time he fighting and screaming. Neighbors listen and then tell everyone we fighting and screaming all the time. Still," she adds wistfully, "even though such *stink*, I miss him."

And in this small way, you think maybe you can soften some of the rougher edges for your mother, just a little bit. You think maybe it's good she's so pissed off. You think maybe it's the thing that's protecting her from being *devastated*, instead.

3. In the Dark Somewhere

Later on, during that first night in Laramie, your mother asks, "What you think your father doing now?"

"I don't know," you say. "What do *you* think he's doing?"

"I think he probably lying by himself in the dark somewhere," she says.

4. Flour

On the way to the funeral home where you've set up an appointment to finalize the cremation arrangements, fill out the necessary paperwork to file the death certificate, and see your father's body one last time, your mother suddenly exclaims, "I so mad about your father for being such *stink* I maybe going to *thwack* him when I see him!" But then she admits, a bit more quietly, "I'm scared to see him."

"I know," you agree. "Me too."

"After this, I never going to see your father again," your mother says. "After today, they going to cook him, and he only going to be flour."

5. Apple

At the funeral home, the staff are competent and kind, and they present your mother with a small marble apple. She thanks them at length, profusely and extravagantly, although you can tell by the expression on her face that she's irritated by the gift. Later, when you're alone in her apartment, she pulls it out of her handbag and rolls her eyes. "What I suppose to do with this?" Then, as has always been her way with disappointing presents over the years, she tosses it onto the floor.

Finally, when the paperwork is complete, the funeral home staff member takes you to the room that's been set up for you and your mother to spend time with your father's body. Although you've been dreading this moment, it comes, strangely, as an unexpected relief. You and your mother both agree that your father looks very much like *himself*, that he looks *peaceful*, as if he's only *asleep*.

Your mother insists you take pictures with your iPhone, and although this makes you feel a bit *uneasy*, you remind yourself that you're here to give your mother anything she needs, or wants, and so you take the pictures. She decides she wants some shots with your father, and so she leans in over his prone body, producing her trademark, dimpled smile—as if posing for a prom photo. She makes you show her the pictures on your iPhone, saying: "This one good one! This no good!" When you get to the pictures of the two of them together, she indignantly asks, "Who this?"

"That's you and my father," you tell her.

"No, it's not!" she insists. "Some strange old man standing next to your father."

She makes you promise to erase all of the pictures with the "strange old man" from your phone.

(You don't.)

Then your mother cries for a while and says she never should have left Japan. "My father, your father's father, your father's brother all dead. Who going to take care of me?"

You promise that you will take care of her, but given that you don't have a penis, this apparently seems anathema to her.

"Oh, Bob!" she sobs dramatically in the direction of your father's body. You realize that your mother's suddenly shifted into her performative public persona, but you're unsure of who she's performing *for* at this moment. "You have to promise you going to watch me from heaven! You have to protect me and take care of me!"

6. Hello

A week into your stay in Wyoming, your mother calls you early in the morning. "Is your father call you on the telephone?" she asks.

"Um, no . . . he didn't?" you say cautiously. "Did he call you?"

"Yes," she says. "He call me on the telephone just now. So I wonder if maybe he call you too."

"What did he say?" you ask, genuinely curious.

"He say *hell-oh*." She says "hello" in a strange sing-song. "But guess what?" she asks.

"What?"

"Now I can't find him anywhere. I look in bathroom. Under covers on bed. Maybe hiding in closet. I don't see him anywhere. Did you see him?"

"No," you say. "I didn't."

You think about phantom limb syndrome. You think about the ache of images of a body missing its life on your iPhone, the ache of a physical body that is now missing too.

7. Unforgiven

On many days, after dinner, your mother reiterates the story of your father and his girlfriends, but on other days, she complains that your father has been mistreated by his doctor.

"She hit him on the head and call him stupid!" your mother says.

"That doesn't sound right," you say. "Remember when she saved his life last year?"

"No! You not here! You don't know! She hit and hit on head so many times. That's why your father have head trouble. Everybody try and push your father down, and you always on their side, not on his side," she says.

"How so?" you ask.

"When doctor tell your father no more drive car you *agree*!"

"Well, it just wasn't safe for him to drive anymore," you say. "I didn't want you to get hurt or killed in a car accident."

"I don't care if we dead in car accident," your mother says. "At least your father be *happy*! He never ever going to forgive you for that."

8. Jealousy

Because your mother keeps bringing up the "nice restaurant" your father took his "girlfriends" to, you make it your mission to treat your mother to lunch at various Laramie restaurants during the month that you're in town. It's a more difficult maneuver than one might initially imagine, because your mother is like the Goldilocks of restaurants. She's always impatient, in a terrible hurry, anxious in unfamiliar settings, upset about the prices, and critical of the food. The first restaurant, a charming downtown bistro, is a wash. Your mother takes two bites of her lunch, pronounces the food at the assisted living center (which she frequently says is "no good") much better, and declares that the restaurant is not her kind of place. The second restaurant, a Thai lunch buffet, fares a little bit better, and your mother finds some noodles that she says taste good, although she objects to the price. The third restaurant is a sushi restaurant across from campus, which she's initially reluctant to try because the sushi restaurant you took her to the previous summer raised her ire due to the "stingy" cuts of fish. This restaurant, though, is just right. “Oh, your father,” she sighs. “He really missing out. He going to be jealous.”

9. Leftovers

“Your father die and we just leftovers,” your mother says to you several days before you have to leave.

You don’t know what to say to her in response.

“Hey!” she insists. “Don’t you think so?”

You shrug, because you don’t want to be a leftover, and you don’t want your mother to think that she’s a leftover, but at the same time, she is also, in a way, brilliantly accurate.

She says it once again: “Now we just leftovers.”

Dear America / Dear Motherland

An Essay in Fractures

1. Aperture

When you die, you want to become all *aperture*, all openness to the rush and heave and teem of the world: the August confetti of the Pleiades spilling down night sky's onyx in a fizzy glitter; the wispy plumes of breath vortexing out from the beaks of small birds' pre-dawn songs; the shape-shifting narratives clouds murmur to the sleeping forms of mountains.

Of course, aperture can also be a kind of rawness, a vulnerability. Lately, each day feels flecked with shrapnel, until it sometimes seems difficult to feel the complexities of one's emotions, only the instinctive animal pain of *woundedness*: images of crying children in cages; photographs of dead whales washing up on beaches in apocalyptic pods; footage of emaciated polar bears stranded on melting ice floes; a car-struck rabbit with a crushed hind leg painfully flailing on asphalt.

Sand chafing raw the tender mollusk within its shell. Grit scraping raw the tender eyeball.

Sometimes you wish to close your eyes and shut everything out, but hypervigilance is both your gift and your curse.

And right now, America makes you want to shutter the lens, close your eyes.

2. Dead Meat

Your mother's brain is coming unraveled from dementia, like a clipped thread of yarn unraveling the complicated cable stitching in a handmade sweater. Some days, you arrive at her apartment to find her in her pajamas, fuming, speaking only Japanese. Some days, she whispers to you that people are listening to her phone conversations because they want to *snitch* her money.

She is *penniless*, she insists, even though your father's left a lifetime of careful savings to her, even though everything they owned was always listed jointly in both your parents' names. In one sense, she's not entirely wrong about her vulnerability: immigrant, non-native speaker of English, Japanese, elderly, woman. At the same time, she's always been taken care of, has always insisted that it's her *right* to be taken care of by someone: her father, your father, now you.

Despite having been a stay-at-home spouse, your mother opted out of many of the domestic responsibilities of being an adult caretaker. She also opted out entirely from the responsibilities of financial caretaking (*i.e.,* accounting, monitoring and paying bills, doing the taxes, planning for retirement, etc.). She coyly referred to financial duties as *important men business*. Yet so much of her daily worries circled around the micromanagement of money. As was her way, she'd opt out of the responsibility, opt out of any understanding of the *mechanics* of fulfilling the responsibility, but then aggressively, furiously, backseat drive.

Every month, your father gave her a budgeted amount of cash with which to run the household: to buy clothes, groceries, and toiletries for the family, to buy things she might personally want or need. But since your mother never seemed to trust that your father was socking away funds into savings or retirement, she'd hoard the monthly cash as tightfistedly as humanly possible, refusing to let it go. You had to beg for permission to wash your hair because a dollop of shampoo was expensive! You had to recycle dirty clothes because laundry soap was expensive! She'd make you carry your lunch to school in a full-size brown paper grocery sack because you couldn't be trusted not to lose your lunchbox and lunchboxes were expensive! She'd only buy meat at the grocery store from the discounted section of recently expired or soon-to-expire meats, which she referred to as the "dead meat section."

Your mother was always fuming about your father, about money—insisting he was spending money she viewed as being rightfully hers. Sometimes she'd describe him as being "not smart about money," while other times she'd call him "a complete stingy." Since his death, your mother frequently reanimates these complaints with deep bitterness. When she's finished excoriating your dead father, she then tractor beams her fury onto you. Her opening salvo: "You even worse than your father!"

3. Forgive and Forget

This complex, toxic family narrative makes people uneasy. Some of your friends and colleagues send you gratingly saccharine emails or DMs anxiously peppered with platitudes and hopes for *forgiveness*. They want a happy ending. But your life right now is messy and complicated. It doesn't adhere to the outlines of a nice narrative, and as far as happy endings go, the abusive mother you're caring for, who failed to care for you, will ultimately die, and there's nothing happy making in *any* of it.

You're having ugly feelings. And you know your well-meaning friends and colleagues *know* you're having ugly feelings. But you feel as if they want to "fix" your ugly feelings or that they want you to have feelings that make *them* feel more comfortable, and you just want to be left in peace to feel your ugly feelings.

Lately, you feel like *forgive and forget*'s a paradigm that aligns too easily with privilege. Your anger, and your memory, are powerful. They help you to process trauma. They help protect you from future abuse. *Forgive and forget* requires exhausting contortions of self-silencing and self-erasure that feel too much to you like *shame*.

Lately, you feel like this current American political moment is similarly messy and complicated. Because doesn't any sort of restorative justice for systemic oppression and epigenetic trauma similarly rely on acknowledging painful truths, acknowledging anger, and refusing to forget histories? You're scared that as a nation, we've erased our own histories to the point that we're doomed to keep repeating them—even at the brink of moral and environmental apocalypse. There's a reason why *Never Forget* is such a prominent phrase on days such as the Day of Remembrance for the Japanese American internment during World War II or on Holocaust Remembrance Day.

You're having a difficult time letting go; it's true. Maybe this makes people uncomfortable because it's somewhat uncharacteristic of you. You usually try to "take the high road," to be open to multiple viewpoints, to compassionately proffer the benefit of the doubt. But increasingly, you feel this relies on the presumption of good faith between parties. You've let go and let go and let go but what it increasingly feels like is that you're letting go of your *self* and that you're giving your *self* away. How can there be any presumption of good faith when it comes to abuse or social injustice or climate change? It makes you consider Karl Popper's paradox of intolerance, in which he asserts that tolerating the intolerant allows the intolerant to destroy the tolerant. It makes you think of different iterations of the John Stuart Mill quote that "liberty consists in the freedom to do everything which injures no one else."

Why must you *always* be the one to forgive? Why must you *always* be the one to forget? Why must you *always* be the one to let go?

4. Gaslight at Sundown

So many things about the Trump administration are triggering, but because of the proximate timeline, you can't help but notice how the toxic gaslighting being spewed from the White House seems so much like the toxic gaslighting from an abusive parent with dementia.

Political/systemic abuse illuminating personal/private abuse and vice versa.

Your mother's obsessively fixated on a narrative of betrayal in which she's the victim and you're the villain. It's like an earworm she can't get out of her head. Every day when you visit, every day when you call her on the phone, there's a point where things turn sour and she becomes angry, accuses you of *snitching* all of her money and giving it to your boyfriend. It eerily parallels the story she tells of your frail and declining father *snitching* the cash she claimed was hidden in their closet at the assisted living center and giving it to his "girlfriend" shortly before his death. It eerily parallels the story she tells about how one of her favorite male nurses *snitched* her jewelry and gave it to his "girlfriend." It eerily parallels the time you were five years old and the catty-corner neighbor gave you a small plate of Oreos to share with your friends, and your mother, who was watching the exchange from her bedroom window, became enraged because she said the cookies were obviously meant for *her*, and instead, you *snitched* them and gave them away to your *brat friends*. You were punished twice: once for stealing and eating the cookies and then once again for lying about the provenance of the cookies.

Over and over again, you gently explain to your mother that, as legal guardian, your job is to protect her money. How all of her money is still *her money*; that it needs to be kept in the bank for *safekeeping*; that legally, you're only allowed to spend her money to pay for *her* care, *her* bills, and *her* expenses. Just like when you were five, your mother insists your explanations are *preposterous lies*.

And nothing you do, in the end, will convince your mother that you're anything other than a *snitcher*, a *liar*, a *thief*. When you show her the court documents, or the bank statements, she says, "Blah, blah, blah, such big talking, I don't care about that!" When you give her large sums of cash for her birthday, or to tide her over for spending money until your next visit, with the caveat that you can arrange to give her more money if she needs it, and that you can also send her any physical items that she needs, she becomes angry because you haven't handed over the *entire estate* to her—all of the savings and investments—*in cash,* to keep under her bed at the assisted living center. She denies that you've ever given her any money at all, piteously claiming that when the other "girls" go to Walmart on the shuttle bus, she has to stay behind because she has no money. You purchase a rechargeable Walmart gift card for her to use—one you can easily re-up from your laptop. A few days later she says she can't even go shopping for *shampoo* because she is *penniless.*

"Your father so upset when I tell him you snitch all my money and give to your boyfriend!" your mother confidentially informs you, sotto voce, inside her apartment. "That's why he tell you don't come, you not welcome, for Christmas before he dead time," she whispers. "He never going to forgive you for that," she says, smiling a little as she goes in for the kill. "Right before he dead time he *hate* you."

5. Narrowing Apertures

You're driving your mother over the Snowy Range. On Saturdays, you try to coax her outside of the assisted living center and take her on outings. As you round the hairpin turns toward the summit—near Mirror Lake and Lake Marie—the peaks, which seem so blue from Laramie, become rocky gray, patterned with tiger stripes of snow. The sky is a grand battle of cloudage: corpulent blue sea beasts versus ruffled dragons of ornately carved white jade.

Your mother seems somewhat happy, recognizing places she used to visit with your father. But when you suggest going back again, several weeks later, she shrugs and says, "I been there two times already! Once with your father and once with you. Why I have to go again?"

You're reminded of driving through Wyoming to summer swim meets. How your mother would insist on rolling up old bath towels, like curtains, into all but the driver's side windows so you wouldn't get *truck-driver suntans.* You imagine the uncountable miles of missed canyon and sky and clouds and prairie and antelope unfurling unseen outside those old bath towels. The way in which your mother has always insisted on maintaining such a narrow aperture to the world troubles you—and now, instead of being a beauty to open her eyes to, you feel like the world will only continue to become increasingly small and narrow. You think of the words *small-minded* and *narrow-minded* and it makes you feel ill.

6. One Candy per Person

An iconic memory of your mother: you are four years old, flying to Arizona to visit your American grandparents over Christmas. Near the end of the flight, the flight attendant circulates through the cabin with a basket of hard candies. Your mother scoops both hands into the basket, attempting to come away with as many shiny candies as she can carry. When the flight attendant makes her put them back, saying she can take only one, your mother is visibly disappointed—agitated and irritable for the rest of the flight.

The house in Laramie is filled to the gills with just this type of hoarded treasure: stale candies, stale tea, stale tins of cookies, expired food, unworn clothes mixed in with trash, mixed in with mountains of plastic bags, mixed in with bill stubs dating back to the 1970s, mixed in with urine-soaked pads, mixed in with an obscene tonnage of mail from the NRA, mixed in with loaded handguns. So many things: unused, unworn, not enjoyed, but mindlessly *accumulated.*

Oh mother, you want to say, thinking of the gleaming, tightly clutched, cellophane-wrapped candies spilling out of her small dimpled hands. *Please let go.*

What a strange foil all of this is to the surreal beauty of the Snowy Range. Thunderheads gather on the horizon in the late afternoon, as you haul things out to the dumpster in front of the house—feeling increasingly sweaty, lonely, furious—and sometimes blue-gray spigots of rain squirt down on the mountains from heavy-bellied clouds as if they were leaky water balloons.

It's a beauty that feels increasingly fragile and evanescent. Each day's news brings new reports of climate change and environmental unraveling: over two hundred reindeer found dead from starvation in Svalbard, Norway; approximately half a billion bees found dead in Brazil, poisoned by the insecticide Fipronil; a memorial held in Iceland for the Okojull glacier, while all of Alaska's sea ice rapidly melts like ice cubes in a too-warm summer cocktail.

You think of America's history of greed and plunder. You think of the atrocities committed for the sake of greed and plunder.

You think of America's sundowning rages when confronted with its oppressive histories.

Oh America, oh motherland, you want to say. *Please, please let go.*

The Unbearable Privilege of Breathing

1. Inspiration

Inspire: to fill with an animating, quickening, or exalting influence. Divinity directly and immediately infused into the mind or soul. But also, the drawing of air, of breath, into the lungs: *inhalation*.

Everything in the world, physical and metaphysical, fueled by breath.

Spires: the apex, or steeple, of buildings; the summit of mountains; the uppermost tapering stalks of trees.

So much reaching, so much desire for sky, air, and breath.

In insects, spiracles are the small spired holes leading to the trachea through which carbon dioxide is exchanged for oxygen. In cartilaginous fish such as skates, rays, and sharks, spiracles create a similar map to the respiratory system. The nasal opening of whales are also called spiracles and facilitate the exchange of carbon dioxide and oxygen into their gigantic, mammalian lungs.

Like photonegative images: cellular respiration takes in oxygen and releases carbon dioxide, while photosynthesis takes in carbon dioxide and releases oxygen. The intricate mapwork of tree roots, branches, stems, leaves, and veins stunningly similar to roots, bronchi, bronchioles, and alveoli of lungs.

(As Frank O'Hara writes, in "Having a Coke with You," *in the warm New York 4 o'clock light we are drifting back and forth / between each other like a tree breathing through its spectacles.*)

Together, all of us simply trying to breathe with and among the trees.

2. Hyponome

Zoom around the spiral's periphery. Your face, their face. Sometimes many faces Brady Bunching. Or like a fever dream of *The Hollywood Squares*, at home sick from school, your lungs on fire, tongue glazed with the sticky sweet of cough syrup.

You are in a fight with the loss of buoyancy, airlessness, deflation. Anger a held-breath tightening in your chest when the downstairs neighbors, who aren't practicing social distancing, roll their eyes when they see you leave in a mask and gloves. The sounds of large house parties down the block late at night. Casual crowds of unmasked shoppers in the grocery store parking lot. Your elderly Japanese mother, whose mind unspirals further from Alzheimer's on a weekly basis, a constant slow leak of grief. And now over one hundred thousand deaths in a little over two months. It's like having the wind kicked out of you. Loss of buoyancy, airlessness, deflation.

(The chambered nautilus uses a siphon, a hyponome, to expel water from the chambers of its shell when it rises to the surface like a gleaming submarine of pearl.)

3. Choke

Such an ugly word for ugliness: disruption of breath through physically crushing or blocking the trachea. Also the disruption of breath through poisoning or contaminating breathable air.

But it's also a strange and nervously jokey word, too. Failure to perform, due to anxiety or nerves is *to choke.*

And *choke* is the diminutive, friendly nickname for artichoke, as well as code for marijuana.

And why is slang for male masturbation—weirdly, disturbingly—sometimes called *choking the chicken*?

But mostly it connotes coughing, gagging, overflow. To obstruct, fill up, clog: like disinformation, like lies, like gaslighting.

It also means to hinder development, progress, and growth: Choke is racism. Choke is corruption. Choke is disaster capitalism. Choke is systemic oppression and institutionally sanctioned genocide.

When we are overcome by emotion, when we fight off tears, we become *all choked up*.

4. Cerebral Hypoxia

With each passing week, your mother's brain becomes increasingly snarled and tangled. She is losing the English language and instead speaks to you in Japanese in a furious whisper over the phone. She accuses you of coming into her room at night and snitching the underwear and compression socks *you purchased for her*. She claims that one of the ladies in her memory care unit is trying to buy her house and that she keeps trying to tell the "head office" she doesn't want to sell. She says she can't talk on the phone to you because everyone is trying to listen in on her conversations so they can snitch all her money.

Scientists have discovered that the amyloid plaques and neurofibrillary tangles of Alzheimer's patients are created by the amyloid-ß protein and that amyloid-ß proteins are commonly associated with cerebral hypoxia, or abnormally low oxygen levels in the brain.

Your mother's brain is slowly choking to death.

Your mother's brain is having trouble breathing.

5. Carapace

Your mother's on lockdown in her assisted living center in Laramie, Wyoming. A plane ride separates you from your sweetheart. Dear friends scattered across the country. It's not that you're exactly rootless, it's more of a lightness in homing, an *untetheredness*. You'd organized your life with a kind of simplicity in mind: the solitude you needed to practice your art and your work, the ability to easily leave for out-of-town poetry readings and artist residencies. For you, these migratory patterns provided you with the personal and artistic connections that kept solitude from hardening into a starker kind of loneliness.

Now you engage in daily epibenthic scavenging of the shelf-stable goods stockpiled on the living room floor of your apartment. Now it's been sixteen weeks since you've touched, or been touched by, another human being.

So you try to focus on small joys. The rain-glazed window blurring the profusion of lilacs outside your window. Shiny grackles that noisily dip themselves into the puddles of water in your alleyway like sheened bread in a fondue pot of cheese. Late afternoon light flaming the paperweights to shimmering prism and iridescence. So many antechambers lustered with nacre.

Your phone pings and chirps and warbles. Constant thrum and drone of tiny robot bees cross-pollinating on social media, transforming <3s into honey.

(the paper chambers flush and fill with light / that comes and goes, like hearts)

6. Iron Lung

A type of negative pressure ventilator that helps the body breathe. During the polio epidemic, iron lungs were used to help ventilate people who couldn't breathe on their own. Some people ended up having to use their iron lungs permanently. A shell of metal carapace. Tender body inside like the squeeze box of an accordion keeping time to its own music.

There are three extant iron lungs still in use today.

If our Earth were to need an iron lung, what would it be? The tiny robo-bees made of drones with horsehair and sticky silica gel?

Or is the Earth already iron lunged: oxygen and fluids and nutrients and excrement artificially extracted, manufactured, and recirculated back through with contaminants?

7. Expire

The termination of a contract, guarantee, or offer.

To breathe out. To exhale air from the lungs.

The extinguishing of a fire.

When the last breath leaves the body.

To die.

8. Ventilation

Exposure to the elements of air and wind.

The infusion of fresh air into a space where the air has become stale or contaminated.

To help a person to breathe, by mechanical assistance, as with a respirator.

When patients become extremely ill with COVID-19, they're placed into a medically induced coma, intubated, and put on a ventilator, which breathes for them. In the most dire circumstances, and if it's available, patients are sometimes placed on an ECMO machine—extracorporeal membrane oxygenation—which will pump and oxygenate their blood outside their body, giving their heart and lungs a chance to rest.

So much time, science, and medical care devoted to help a human being continue breathing. All of it so easily snuffed out by racist guns, by a torturous chokehold, by the murderous knee to the back of a neck.

Is hate a virus?

And if so, would anti-vaxxers insist on refusing the inoculation?

9. Antechambered

At night, when you can't sleep, you turn to the hypnotic slosh of the waves along the shoreline of your deserted island on Animal Crossing. You run up and down the beach in your green rubber boots, fishing. It self-soothes the rising tides of anxiety, distracts you from the pending hurricanes of depression. You exchange gifts with your sweet, but odd, animal villagers: Genji the rabbit asks if you'd like to buy his skeleton. Hazel the squirrel reminds you to look up at the stars.

In the meantime, the cats grow plumper from extra treats and full-time cosseting. They are so plush. And warm. Because there are days when you feel like a balloon floating away on a cut string, you let them weigh you down with their increasing *tangibilities*.

In the meantime, you call your mother every day, even though she is always furious with you. When you ask her how she is, she sometimes says, *I hate you, Lee Ann Roripaugh, is how I am*. She likes to hang up the phone on you. Sometimes you call her back and she picks up the phone and shouts, *Nobody home!*

And this is exactly how *you* are sometimes: sealed and bell-jarred tight in your innermost chamber, absenting yourself from the muscular, depressive torque of your own downward-spiraling thoughts: *Nobody home!*

But still, you rise—and you rise again—in all of your wobbly buoyancy. The recursivity of spiraling.

(*the paper chambers flush and fill with light / that comes and goes, like hearts*)

So many antechambers lustered with nacre.

10. Respire

To breathe. To inhale and exhale air for the purpose of maintaining life.

The police keep murdering our citizens, and our cities are choked with virus and flame.

Respiration used to be so easy, so transparent, for so many people. Now it is has become material. An increasingly commodifiable luxury. A privilege.

Can re-spiration be transformative, like re-vision?

I can breathe easy again, we like to say, after a period of anxiety or trouble. To breathe easy again at this moment seems unimaginably distant. And yet. (And yet.) As Plath writes in her poem "Tulips," *I am aware of my heart: it opens and closes / Its bowl of red blooms out of sheer love of me. / The water I taste is warm and salt, like the sea, / And comes from a country far away as health.*

Breath in. Breath out.

Our hearts opening and closing.

Oxygen in. Carbon dioxide out.

Re-spire.

Dream of a Two-Headed Turtle

1.

Late October, and you notice an ominous bubbling on social media. An emotional cratering, a hot spot. Slow roil and scald of lava spilling over. A silent knife of electronic keening, the glib invective of virtual rubberneckers passing by. At the molten core, you discover the grisly truth: one of your Facebook friends, Michele, a woman you knew growing up in Laramie, Wyoming, now a psychologist, has murdered her twin seven-year-old daughters before committing suicide.

How do you imagine the unimaginable? And yet, any sort of proximity to the unimaginable forces one to attempt to try and make sense of incoherence. To try and wrap one's brain like a dampening woolen blanket around the contours of a person you once knew and didn't realize was on fire, manifesting the flame and fear and pain and damage that lie below.

But she is gone. Which means the person you are searching out beneath the blanket is you. And the fire that you manifest is your own fire.

2.

How you first meet: You and Michele are competing in a local piano competition, and there's some thorniness, or obstruction. Both of you are maybe twelve, or thirteen. You win first place in the piano competition, and Michele wins second place. But then Michele's father objects to the results. He insists on speaking to the judges. After a half hour of whispered consultation, the judges decide to overturn their original results and declare a tie instead. You and Michele are then named co-winners of the piano competition.

Your parents smile and smile, but back at home, they erupt into a monthslong tailspin of private conspiracy, invective, rage. Michele's father, they insist, is *in cahoots* with the judges. They deride Michele's piano playing. They mock her appearance. When they become weary of demonizing Michele, they turn their diatribe toward you. What was the matter with *you*? Why didn't you play *better*? Why didn't you play well enough to make sure you came in *first place* instead of a *tie*?

Decades later, on Facebook, Michele suggests that her father was a narcissist, and in her family dynamic, she was the golden child, her brother the scapegoat. Is this the moment in which you clearly realize, that as an only child, you were required to simultaneously function as both golden child in public and scapegoat in private?

3.

Two weeks after the murder-suicide, the 2020 presidential elections are called for Joe Biden and Kamala Harris. In response, Trump goes on national television and declares himself the winner instead. Beginning the stupidest of stupid coups, he rolls out, for the first time, his baseless accusations of election fraud, which he will continue repeating and Tweeting on a daily basis: inciting violence, bullying his party members into seditious acts, and fleecing his misbegotten flock of bigoted and QAnon-addled sheep into donating hundreds of millions of dollars.

It's sickening for all the obvious reasons, but part of your queasiness is that you grew up in a house with a mother who was, by your best guess, an undiagnosed narcissist with borderline personality disorder. You were regularly bullied into telling lies in public that would conform to a false narrative constructed by your mother. You were regularly bullied into having to acknowledge things that were factually untrue as being true. *This* feels too much like *that.*

4.

When Michele turns up in your eighth-grade class at the university lab school, you're both assigned to play piano in jazz band. She's a shy beanpole of a girl, long-fingered hands covered with a light dusting of freckles. You sit next to one another on the piano bench in the basement band room, sharing the piano parts. She smiles easily, and there's a sweetness, an openness there, with what sometimes feels like a brief flicker of bewilderment at the core.

You could have been friends. Two bespectacled girls with braces and headgear who loved music. Both gentle. Both, as it will eventually turn out, pansexual. At the time you felt she was *nicer* than you. Your parents, who constantly shamed you for being "thin-skinned," who could sense a propensity for *milquetoastiness* about you in the same way sharks sense blood in the water, were always trying to strop you into a honed knife blade. Everything a competition. Everyone a threat.

Decades later, when you reconnect on Facebook, you compare notes about the obligatory performativity of the "golden child"—the hiding of self, the buried anxiety. You lament the friendship that could have been. *And oh how we both needed a kindred spirit <3* she writes to you in your DMs.

5.

In the weeks following the election, COVID-19 continues to decimate the nation, rages unchecked through your state. You're afraid to leave your apartment. Your governor, who insisted on hosting multiple superspreader events throughout the summer and fall such as the Sturgis Motorcycle Rally and who you spitefully like to refer to as the Trumplicker-in-Chief, refuses to even *consider* a statewide mask mandate. Any possible edge South Dakota might have had with respect to the virus (open rural spaces, time to learn and prepare, low population density) completely squandered away—leaving behind economically vulnerable communities, vulnerable Native American communities, and a medical system that's being stretched perilously thin.

You know and recognize this sense of feeling stuck, cornered, trapped in an abusive situation. Yet even your instinctive trauma responses are constrained. Sometimes you can lose yourself in work, in Netflix, in Animal Crossing, but eventually you find yourself backed into a corner again. On a near-daily basis, suicidal ideation floats idly by like a temporary thought, a cool-shadowed cloud. You tell yourself that it's the existence of *choice* that's important. That it's only a *metaphor* for flight. Then, patiently, you make yourself wait for the fog and mists of depression to clear the room.

6.

In high school, Michele changes. She escapes what she will later describe to you as "forced piano playing." In contrast, you throw yourself obsessively into music, practicing six to eight hours a day. You get up at 4:00 in the morning to practice before school, and you practice after school until it's time for dinner. For you, the piano playing isn't forced. What's forced is the crushing obligation (no excuses!) to *win* every single piano competition. For you, music is a form of escape. A kind of daydreaming, a disassociation, a way of absenting yourself from your body and existing elsewhere, inside a lustrous shell of Chopin, Debussy, and Ravel.

Your last memory of Michele from Laramie is at the Skyline Skate roller rink: glasses and braces gone, her hair bird-winged into brown feathered waves, roller skates adorned with huge pink fuzzy pom-poms as she circles the rink under the glittering sparks of a disco mirror ball.

7.

Your mother's assisted living facility in Laramie is under lockdown because of COVID-19, and you haven't been able to visit in nearly a year. Lately, during your daily phone calls, she's taken to asking how many children you have. When you tell her you don't have any children, she becomes angry, calls you a liar. She says that you have *three children*. She knows because she's *seen* you with them. She accuses you of selling her house and giving all of her money to *your three stink brats*. Then she tells you what a useless and horrible person you are and hangs up the phone.

Of course, you understand much of this is the Alzheimer's. Of course, you understand it's best to just sit with the person *inside* their delusion and go along with it. Not to argue. Not to try and ply them with logic.

And even though you know all this, for some reason, you *balk* at agreeing with your mother that you have three children that you don't actually *have*.

Maybe because it's an *accusation*. Maybe it's because her uncanny grandchildren aren't a source of pleasure or happiness but targets she wants to burn down with paranoid Molotov cocktails of rage. Maybe because there's something within you that insists on protecting these children of delusion. Maybe because you'd rather absorb them back into your own body than subject them to your mother's (grand)mothering.

8.

You remember experiencing a slight pang of envy when, at forty-eight, after a whirlwind romance, Michele married, then became pregnant with her twins, Mairy and Katie. Her joy was palpable.

And it's not that you even *wanted* those things for yourself, per se, it was more the occasional small hot flicker of worry that it was damage from abuse that made you *not* want those things *more*.

And yet, when the unraveling comes, it comes quickly and hard. The divorce acrimonious, dragging on endlessly, with multiple hearings, and ugly child-custody disputes. Michele outspoken in her belief that her estranged husband's a toxic narcissist. She files a restraining order against him for domestic violence. She's convinced he's been sexually abusing the seven-year-old twins. As the divorce wears on, she expresses frustration over the ease with which he seems to win over the goodwill of lawyers, judges, and social workers. In his counternarrative, Michele is "the crazy one," and as she becomes increasingly desperate, her edges begin to fray, and her own struggles with depression surface. Several days after a court hearing in which Michele's request for sole custody is denied in favor of joint custody, Michele gives the girls heavy doses of sedatives, then places them in her bed. She shoots them both in the head before turning the gun on herself.

9.

Day after excruciating day of watching the COVID-19 death toll rise. Day after excruciating day of being subjected to an unhinged national gaslighting. You find it difficult to sleep, and your dreams become increasingly turbulent.

In the opening of *Anna Karenina*, Tolstoy wrote, "All happy families resemble one another; each unhappy family is unhappy in its own way." What was Tolstoy getting at, you sometimes wonder. Was he gesturing, for example, at something like Winnicott's theory of the "good enough mother"? At the seemingly banal yet crucial aspects of safety, support, affection? Was he perhaps also suggesting that no one can truly understand the full contours of an abusive relationship, a dysfunctional family, unless they've suffocated within the closed doors of that particular toxic sphere?

Once again, how do you imagine the unimaginable?

In one of your dreams you're being chased by ICE agents. You hide inside a bathroom stall, holding your breath, dreading discovery. Somehow, you manage to escape and find yourself running outside, through woods. You're near a stream. You see a turtle in the leaves. When you gently pick it up and hold it in the palm of your hand, you discover that it's a *two-headed turtle*.

You think of two girls playing four-handed piano. You think of Michele's twins. You think of yourself, failed golden child and belligerent scapegoat, retracted inside the shell of your apartment, nursing your griefs.

When you Google dream interpretations, you learn that a dream of hiding from authorities indicates shame or guilt. Wishing there was something you could have done. You learn that dreaming of a two-headed turtle represents domestic bliss, inner nourishment. A gentle exterior with a fierce and resilient interior. A relinquishment of control over the embodied self. A foreshadowing of a time of freedom, tranquility, and renewal.

Lost in Translation

1. Manicure

When your mother's found wandering in her pajamas on the street in the snow outside her assisted living center in the middle of the night, she's moved to the locked ward in memory care the very next day.

How they do it: Because she seems to enjoy getting her nails done, they call in the manicurist to give her a special manicure in the afternoon after lunch. During that time, movers come and rapidly transfer all of the belongings from her apartment to the room she's been assigned in the memory care wing of the assisted living center. Then they transport the overflow offsite into a local storage locker.

After that, staff members escort her to her new room in memory care.

Your mother accuses you of playing a dirty trick on her and she isn't entirely wrong.

2. Japanglish Ga Hanase Masu Ka?

Shortly after the move to memory care, your mother's English, which has become increasingly spotty, begins to rapidly disappear in increasingly large chunks. You feel a similar dismay to the dismay you feel when watching graphic simulations of melting polar ice caps.

Like a rising tide, the percentage of Japanese she speaks in each phone conversation spills over a little more with each passing day. The problem is you *don't* speak Japanese. You used to, as a toddler, but then your mother abruptly stopped speaking Japanese to you. The story is that you couldn't keep things straight, that you were confusing the neighbors with your Japanglish.

But later on, when you wanted to take Japanese in college, your parents made you take French instead because you'd taken French in high school. Besides, your mother insisted, Japanese was *too hard* and you were *too stupid* and you might get a *bad grade*! After graduate school, when you attempted to teach yourself how to speak Japanese using Rosetta Stone software, your mother mercilessly mocked your basic, childish sentences.

In retrospect, what you notice is a pattern where your mother cuts off, or deliberately obstructs, the venues by which you might effectively communicate with one another. Most recently, when you call her in the afternoon each day, she likes to yell at you in Japanese before slamming down the phone.

3. Discharged

A few weeks after the move to memory care, after COVID-19 has forced the facility to go into complete lockdown, your mother tells you that somebody's trying to *kick her out*! That somebody wants to buy her house and then she will have *nowhere to go*! Again and again, you *promise* her that she's not going to be kicked out of her assisted living center, that no one's going to sell her house.

After your father's death, you'd volunteered to sell the house in Wyoming and move your mother to South Dakota. But she insisted that without the house she had *nothing*. She made you *promise* not to sell her house. It's the last choice she was able to make with any sort of clarity.

A week later, and your mother's still insisting that the woman at her assisted living center is trying to *kick her out*, is threatening to *buy her house*. This apparently escalates until one day your mother reports that they had *a big screaming match*.

Later that afternoon, the assisted living center calls, requesting permission to move your mother to a different room in memory care. They say there's a woman who used to be a registered nurse, who thinks she's still at the hospital. The former registered nurse likes to stop by the rooms of the other residents and prepare them for discharge. They say she seems to be upsetting your mother, and they think your mother's quality of life will be better if she's moved to a different pod, away from the woman who used to be a registered nurse.

You agree, because what choice do you have, really, and so your mother's moved (again) to a different room, in another pod, in memory care.

Your mother, of course, is furious with you. It takes a few days for the phone transfer to go through, and when you're able to speak again, your mother accuses you of *selling her house* so you can keep all her nice things for yourself. She describes a nefarious plot in which you're living it up now—wearing all her nice pajamas, all of her nice shoes.

4. In Cahoots with the Duolingo Owl

Because you know staff members and residents at the assisted living center couldn't understand your mother even *before* she started reverting to her native Japanese and because you find it intolerable that no one understands what your mother is trying to say, you begin learning emergency Japanese on Duolingo.

At first, you imagine that if you're able to identify Japanese words you might be able to at least map the general direction of your mother's thoughts and fill in the rest through intuitive guesswork. You remind yourself that, as a child, you sat through entire Japanese tea parties where your mother and her guests would address you in Japanese, and you would answer in English.

But you discover you can sometimes use Japanese as a crowbar to crack open torrents of speech from your mother. In Japanese, you ask your mother if she's well, or you inquire about the weather, and then you just let her speak. You frequently can't keep up, and you mostly fake it by interjecting polite responses (*So desu, yo ne?*) at the appropriate times. What seems important, though, is that your mother can talk as long and as much as she wants and that maybe she will feel, at least in some small way, *heard*.

5. Her Sister's Socks

One day, staff members call to say there's been an incident involving your mother. Apparently, they caught her removing another resident's *socks* and taking them away from the man, a wheelchair user, leaving him in his bare feet.

They say your mother kept insisting they were her *sister's socks* and that the wheelchair-using resident had *snitched* them. Although they escort your mother back to her room, she's soon back out in the common area, removing the wheelchair-using resident's socks again.

The aides escort her back to her room a second time. Apparently, your mother and the wheelchair-using resident, whose socks your mother keeps trying to abscond with, have now both become quite agitated.

Your mother, who's nothing if not recalcitrant, returns for yet a third time to remove and take away the wheelchair-using resident's socks. This time, however, the wheelchair-using resident has grabbed your mother by the wrist and is threatening to "clock her one" by the time the aides arrive.

It's baffling of course. Because your mother usually says that you are her *sister*, you wonder if she thinks the socks resemble the stash of socks you purchased for her the last time you were in Laramie, which she promptly hid within the mouse's nest of her bedroom. At the same time, you've noticed an increasing slipperiness between *my father* (meaning your father, her deceased husband) and *my sister* (meaning you, her daughter, although you sometimes suspect that she conflates you with a sister who once borrowed her silk stockings without her permission). And then, eerily, you wonder if the man is wearing socks that resemble the socks your deceased father used to wear.

6. People Such Stupid

As COVID-19 surges and the year begins to wane, the daily phone calls break down altogether. They only seem to trigger a feedback loop of rage for your mother, and so you stop calling. When you call on Thanksgiving, she tells you how horrible you are and hangs up the phone. When you call on Christmas, she tells you how much she hates you and hangs up the phone. You wait a few weeks, then set up weekly Zoom calls facilitated by the memory care staff.

On the first Zoom call, you immediately become aware that your mother doesn't recognize you because she ostentatiously compliments your skin: *such smooth! such young-looking! such white!*

You know she doesn't know it's you because, historically speaking, she unrelentingly criticizes your skin. Plus, you recognize it as one of the over-the-top compliments she uses to, as she puts it, *butter people up*. As the Alzheimer's has progressed, you've seen her increasingly rely on this particular brand of social lubricant, with strange results: The nurse with rosacea, who looks slightly bewildered and uncomfortable. Betty, who's in her nineties and clearly DGAF and probably never GAF about that kind of thing anyways.

While there's a lavishly unsettling hyperbole about the compliments regarding complexion, what bothers you the most isn't the (mis)calculation of friendship. It is, after all, tempting to be touched by your mother's attempts to reach out, to connect, to exchange pleasantries. What bothers you, instead, is the profound insincerity, the astonishing cynicism.

Because without fail, anytime your mother complimented someone's skin in front of you, once they were out of earshot, her smiling expression would completely change and she'd say, "See how happy she is? Even when such complete *ugly* but you tell them they have beautiful skin and they so *happy*!" Then, she'd sometimes mutter, as an afterthought, "People such *stupid*."

Still, when your mother, for the first time in over a year, expresses delight to see you, as she tells you how *beautiful* your skin is, even as you know that she has no idea who you are, you can't help but glow under the predatory searchlight of her demented charm.

Yup, you think to yourself. *People such stupid.*

7. Crushing It

But worse than the days when your mother doesn't recognize you are the days in which your mother *does* recognize you on Zoom. Her entire body language changes: hostile, combative, bored.

She tells you how *useless* you are. What a bad daughter and horrible person you are. She says she has nothing to say to you. And since she can't hang up the phone on you, she says she's going to *crush it*.

Then she closes shut the staff member's laptop with the open Zoom session. And *crushes it*.

8. Missed Connections

Things you wish you could tell her, if you could:

The sparrow that's hollowed out a cubby in the rotten wood at the edge of an upstairs window. How you can hear the soft whir of its feathers—its chirps and tweets and rubbery squeaks.

The rare kabocha squash that arrived in your food box, that you will roast in a glaze of miso, honey, and shoyu.

How the other day you remembered the time she bought a yellow watermelon at the farmer's market so that she could "trick" your father.

How you know that she must be lonely, which is why you keep calling, even though she keeps hanging up on you, even though she keeps *crushing* you.

How you know this because you are lonely too.

Austere and Lonely Offices

1. Everything Is on Fire

You arrive in Laramie in early July. After several filmy days—instead of the searing blue clotted by the slow heft of extravagant clouds typical for late summer in Wyoming—you realize it's haze caused by smoke from the Pacific Northwest fires. The mountains aren't even visible, the sky an occluded cataract. Everything's too hot and everything's on fire. You feel like a dumbstruck lobster in the pot, claws scuttling the metal sides.

Before rain, you can smell ozone and smoke. The weather app on your phone chirps red exclamation points with every thunderstorm: fire danger from lightning strikes, flash flood watches, and warnings about burn scar mud slides in the Snowy Range. It occurs to you there's a terrible electrical fire taking place in your mother's brain as well—leaving gray burn scars that are easily oversaturated and prone to flooding. Like a startled owl, she peers at you from behind her smudged glasses, muttering in nonstop Japanese, as she tries to figure out how to close the door to her room but can't.

2. All Plug Up

You usually arrive at the memory care center an hour before lunch to sit with your mother and keep her company while she eats. She's been losing weight again. In memory care, staff members circle the dining room during lunch, cajoling the finicky eaters to take a few more bites of this or that. Your mother slumps in her chair like a petulant child, says she doesn't want to eat, tries to pawn her lunch off onto you.

Before she was moved to memory care, before she lost most of her English, your mother became convinced that vegetables were making her "all plug up," that her doctor had told her she shouldn't eat them. Every time you tried to convince her otherwise, she'd get mad and say you didn't know what you were talking about. In the end this was not the hill you were prepared to die on.

So you ignore the vegetables and point to untouched items on her plate, mentally calculating which of them might be the most calorically dense, and plead with her to at least take a couple of bites.

Kore? she asks. *This one?*

Kore to kore, kudasai, you reply. *This one and this one, please.*

She sighs, takes a single unenthusiastic bite off the end of her knife. At the end of the meal, the nurse, who's quietly assessed the amount of food remaining on your mother's plate, comes around with your mother's meds and has her wash them all down with a cup of Ensure.

3. Please Help

At the next table over, Rosella intones her inevitable lunchtime refrain: *Help me*, she says, again and again. *Somebody please help me.* The nursing assistants and nurses cut up Rosella's food, place her spoon back in her hand, and remind her that she can feed herself. Although you wish someone would just go and help Rosella out, you understand there are other factors at stake: Whether or not Rosella has enough ADLs in place to remain in the facility's memory care center, or if she might need to be transferred to the dismal and short-staffed local nursing home if she's no longer able to feed herself. Whether or not Rosella might require a feeding assistant to come in and feed her, which might or might not be covered by Medicare or Medicaid. Whether or not Rosella would develop the increased risks of aspiration or choking common in people with dementia who aren't in control of their own feeding. And yet it's hard to remain immune to her plaintive cries, which increase in volume over the course of the meal: *Please help. Somebody please help me.*

You prefer the days when Rosella's feeling *salty*. One day you hear her drawl, very slowly, very deliberately: *Kiss my ass!*

Another day, she looks a staff member straight in the eyes and says, *Goddamn fuckass!*

4. Pay to Play

You try to never come empty-handed. You bring flowers, gifts, items that your mother requests or needs, but the only thing that seems to make her happy is an envelope stuffed full of cash.

She's not allowed to handle real money anymore and doesn't have the capacity to safely leave the memory care center, so you've become a connoisseur of fake movie-set money. You hand the fake money off to her in $1,000 increments, $5,000 in her birthday card. You briefly consider bringing in a huge bag full of "cash" to her, drug-dealer style, but decide against it because she'll forget that it happened, sometimes within a matter of hours. It's admittedly less fraught than when you used to give her real money, none of which she ever spent anyways, but it's still emotionally exhausting.

Any conversation can quickly derail into angry accusations that you've come into her room at night and *snitched* all her money. You keep an envelope at the ready in your handbag so that at the first mention of the word "money" you can pull out the envelope and give it to her. For a small moment in time, your mother seems happy as she counts out the one-hundred-dollar bills: *hyaku, hyaku, hyaku.* When she asks how many *hyaku* and you say *sen hyaku yen desu*, she makes of her mouth a small delighted "oh." And then like Eeyore, in the chapter from *Winnie the Pooh* titled "In Which Eeyore Has a Birthday and Gets Two Presents," she transfers the money, in an obsessive circuit, from envelope to plastic sack to wrapped napkins in her underwear drawer back to the envelope again.

One day, you're in a rush and forget to put an envelope of "cash" in your handbag. You immediately regret it because, upon your arrival, your mother pulls you into her room then whispers that she doesn't have any money! You tell her you will bring her money *ashita*, tomorrow. She says your husband won't like that. You tell her you don't have a husband, that you have a good job, and that you will bring her money, *ashita*. Your mother becomes angry then and asks if you have a job, why haven't you given her any money? She doesn't have a job! She doesn't have any money! What's the matter with you? You have a job, and you've never given her any money!

You gently suggest that if she looks in her purse, she'll find envelopes with the "money" you've given her. "No," she says. "You just want to try and snitch it." You promise you won't touch the money, that you just want her to check her handbag. She opens the turn-lock clasp on her purse and starts handing you items from inside: used Kleenex, used napkins, two pieces of toast from breakfast wrapped in toilet paper. When you hand the toast back to her, she says you should eat the toast, and when you say *Iie, kekkou desu*, she unwraps the toast, jauntily takes a bite from one of the pieces, then winds it back in the toilet paper and returns it to her purse. Finally, she unearths one of the cash envelopes. You tell her to look inside, but she refuses and, instead, tries to hide the envelope behind her on the bed. "No. That's nothing," she says. "Nobody give me any money, not one penny, since your father die time."

5. "What Did I Know, What Did I Know / of Love's Austere and Lonely Offices?"

It's not that you want or need or even expect credit, exactly, it's that the credit, when given, always goes to somebody else.

For example, your mother gestures at the wreath you purchased for her door and tells you it's pretty. When you say you're happy she thinks so, she tells you that your father made it for her before he died.

After lunch, in her room, she points at the flowers on her dresser that you bought for her and tells you that "some nice boy"—she didn't know who he was—gave them to her.

She shows you the new ASICS you sent to her, says they're very good shoes: *totemo yoi kutsu*. When you say you're glad she likes them and ask if they fit okay, she tells you of course they fit okay because her father, your Japanese grandfather, made them for her.

Your sweetheart flies to Laramie for a long weekend and when you take him to meet your mother, you bring her a fresh bouquet of flowers. You offer to let him present them to her, but he demurs, saying you should be the one to give them to her. You joke that because he has a penis, he's going to get the credit anyways. You both laugh about this, but sure enough, when you return to see your mother at the assisted living center the next day, after driving your sweetheart back to the airport, your mother points at the flowers and says your brother came to visit and brought her flowers.

(*Have you mentioned you're an only child?*)

Maybe it's not even about getting credit. Maybe it's that once you're back in South Dakota for the fall semester, you know your mother will go back to saying you never do anything for her, that you're *a complete useless*, an idiot daughter, and despite your best efforts, you'll feel shitty about this because you're just sort of *milquetoasty* that way.

When you drove over the familiar peaks and bends of the Snowy Range during your sweetheart's visit—the snow-capped crown of blue that tiaras the horizon and always makes you feel a pinched clench of *homesickness* inside—you showed him the spot where you saw the moose three summers before.

You'd been at an artist residency at Brush Creek Ranch outside Saratoga, and for the duration, all the other residents—the painters, composers, and writers, some from as far away as Maryland and New York State—wistfully expressed their desire to see a moose. They used the shy, hushed tones you imagined being used by the passengers on the bus in Elizabeth Bishop's poem "The Moose."

And even though there were antelope, bald eagles, embarrassingly tame deer, and a hedgehog that liked to spy on the composers through their studio windows, the other residents ended up being whisked away by the airport shuttle without ever having seen a moose. But as you drove yourself back to Laramie later that morning on the Snowy Range Road, you spotted something—massive, brown, shaggy—in your peripheral vision, and you realized it was a female moose. You quietly pulled over, cut the engine. You looked and looked, holding your breath. Then, as you slowly reached into the back seat for your camera, the moose bounded off—knobby kneed and awkward—into the forest. It was a moment that filled you with joy. But it also made you unreasonably lonely.

Because if no one else is even *there* to witness the moose, or *remember* the moose, is it—like love, or maybe like kindness, even—only a shambling figment of your imagination?

My Sister's Keeper

An Essay of Unbraiding

Your mother calls you her sister, and it's a slippage that's both linguistic and cognitive.

It happens for the first time at the doctor's office. You're serving as an ad hoc translator between your mother and her gerontologist. At one point, an errant strand of hair falls across your mother's face and you gently tuck it back into place. *She my sister*, your mother tells her doctor. *Big bossy sister.*

Splitting—adjective:
(1) being split or causing something to split.
(2) violent or severe, as a headache.
(3) very fast or rapid.

During the time you stay with your mother in the house while your father's being rehabbed in the nursing home, she sometimes talks about her Onē-san. "Nobody believe we sisters!" she'd exclaim. "We look complete different. So at school, I never tell anybody we sisters. Pretend like I don't even know her."

In one memory from Japan, she describes how her sister was perpetually late. Your mother always arrived at the train platform early, in plenty of time to catch the train for school. But then at the very last minute, her sister would come running over the hill.

Running, waving, and yelling: *Wait for me! Wait for me!* Sometimes your mother laughs when she shares this anecdote. Other times, she relates the narrative in tight tones of disgust, adding that her sister *had no shame.*

Splitting—noun:
4. a part or fragment that has been split off from something.

A tale of two kimonos: Your mother and her sister were allowed to choose material for new kimonos. Your mother describes the pattern that she selected as simple, quiet, traditional, *elegant.* Your mother describes the pattern that her sister selected as modern, bright, *crazy.* When your mother tells this story, it's very clear which choice is the right kimono choice and which choice is the wrong one. Your mother always concludes by saying that you're *exactly* like her sister.

splitting (APA Dictionary of Psychology):
n.
1. In Kleinian analysis and Fairbairnian theory, a primitive defense mechanism used to protect oneself from conflict, in which objects provoking anxiety and ambivalence are dichotomized into extreme viewpoints that fluctuate in extremes of seeing the self or others as either all good or all bad. This mechanism is used not only by infants and young children, who are not yet capable of integrating these polarized viewpoints, but also by adults with dysfunctional patterns of dealing with ambivalence; it is often associated with borderline personality disorder. Also called ***splitting of the object****.*

Your mother frequently sets herself up as the *good one*: the rule follower, the popular one, the favorite daughter and granddaughter. Her sister, she used to say, was the *troublemaker*. And yet your mother was the one who eloped to America with a Yankee after a secret courtship.

Years later, she will describe her life as *such horrible*. She will say she regrets having left Japan. She will say she only did it because she felt *sorry* for your father. That because he'd borrowed money to come back to Japan again after having been discharged from the army, what choice did she have? She will imply that she thought your father was a *country bumpkin*. She will say if she'd stayed in Japan, her family would be taking good care of her.

At the same time, you remember how, in an unguarded moment, she once confided that in Japan, the plan for her was to take over her grandmother's finishing school for rural girls and that there was talk of a match with a young man who she scathingly described as a *country bumpkin*.

splitting (APA Dictionary of Psychology):

n.

2. in cotherapy, divisiveness that a client provokes between therapists to polarize them on treatment decisions and to undermine the therapeutic process. Also called ***splitting situation****.*

While your father's being rehabbed in the nursing home, your mother talks nonstop about what a *horrible* person he is. She keeps returning to the time after they'd eloped and she joined him in New Mexico, where he was working on a master's degree. Your mother says that when she told him he was *stingy*, he suggested that she could get a job. A *job*!!! Mostly, though, she seems personally betrayed by your father's rapid decline in health and ability. The shift in roles from *caretaken* to *caretaker*. Her vitriol is so vehement you secretly debate whether or not your parents should even be living together.

About four months after you move your parents into assisted living, after a brief period of calm, your mother starts needling your father again. She keeps reminding him that after the diagnosis of stroke and vascular dementia, you'd consulted with his doctor about having his driver's license revoked. She convinces your father that you've absconded with all of their savings. That you're going to sell their house and keep all the money. Unless they need you to send them things or make arrangements on their behalf, they hang up the phone on you when you call. Your father tells you they don't want to see you, that you're not welcome.

Splitting—intransitive verb:
(1a) : to become split lengthwise or into layers
(1b) : to break apart : BURST
(2a) : to become divided up or separated off
// split into factions
// split from the group
(2b) : to sever relations or connections : SEPARATE
(2c) : LEAVE
especially : to leave without delay
// split for the coast

About eight months after you move your parents into assisted living, your father falls in the bathroom. He strikes his head and dies of a catastrophic cerebral hemorrhage. You return to Laramie to take care of things and comfort your mother. Your mother resumes the triangulation—only now your *father* is the horrible one again, the abandoning ghost. She complains that all he ever wanted to do was have *big screaming matches* with her. She says he snitched all the money she'd hidden in their closet and gave it to his new girlfriend.

splitting hairs : to make oversubtle or trivial distinctions

As your father's presence fades and the family starts to come unbraided, Onē-san permanently enters the picture. At first, your mother just calls you her "sister." *This my sister* she says to people at the assisted living center. *Talk to my sister*, she says when asked a question that she doesn't understand. Mostly, it seems like a linguistic slippage.

Shortly after your mother's dementia worsens and she's moved to memory care, COVID-19 hits. As the pandemic wears on, you become aware that your mother's split you into two people: a benevolent older sister who takes care of her and the horrible daughter. Occasionally, over Zoom, your mother calls you Onē-san, older sister. In hushed tones, she complains about her idiot daughter, who's snitched all her money, who never does anything for her. Other times, over Zoom, she archly mentions that Onē-san sent her flowers, a birthday present, new shoes. Mostly, though, she calls you a *complete useless* and accuses you of various types of malfeasance, before she "crushes" the Zoom call by slamming the laptop shut.

It will be over a year before your mother's assisted living center reopens to visitors, before you complete your course of COVID-19 vaccines and are able to safely travel. When you finally see your mother in person again, you have no idea what to expect. You arrive with flowers and presents. *Tadaima, Okaa-san*, you say. You're prepared for her to reject you as she does on Zoom, but surprisingly, she doesn't. Later on, she will ask if you've seen her sister. She will make sure no one's listening outside her door, then lower her voice to a whisper. She will warn you to *watch out* for Onē-san. *Don't tell her anything*, your mother says. *She's such troublemaker.*

Family Portrait Over Time in Binary:

110

101

110

10(1)

11 (0)

10(1)

(1)0

0

(0)

Sometimes you imagine your mother as a young girl in Japan, in her sailor-collared school uniform, waiting impatiently for the train in Ota City. She is early and you are not. You come running over the hill as fast as you can while everyone boards the train. *Wait for me! Wait for me!* you call, waving frantically. But you're always already too late. The train pulls away from the boarding station. Your mother's looking directly at you from her window. Maybe she doesn't recognize you. Maybe she's pretending she doesn't know you. Maybe she doesn't even see you at all.

The Atomic Age

1. Drop the Bomb

After your mother elopes with your father on August 6, 1955, the tenth anniversary of the dropping of the atomic bomb on Hiroshima, your father returns by himself to Albuquerque, New Mexico, where he's working on a master's degree in English at the University of New Mexico. Your mother goes home to, as she says, "drop the bomb" on her family.

Several months later, following a bureaucratic tangle of paperwork (in which your mother indignantly complains that the Office of Immigration tries to make her get the required vaccinations for *Mexico* as opposed to *New* Mexico), your mother flies to America on Japan Airlines. She follows the wooden crates sent by ship ahead of time—packed with hand-painted silk kimonos, the Western-style dresses and suits sewn for your mother by her tailor in Ota City, the bespoke Western-style leather shoes made for her in her father's shoe store, and a copy of *The American Way of Housekeeping*. There's a stopover in Honolulu Airport in Hawaii, where your mother has to present her paperwork, marriage certificate, as well as an X-ray of her lungs to prove she doesn't have tuberculosis.

Because the logo for Japan Airlines is a red crane and your mother once showed you her plane tickets to America and because there's a framed Japanese wood-block print above the living room sofa titled

"Woman Riding a Crane" by Suzuki Harunobu, you imagine, as a small child, that your mother came to America riding on the back of a crane. You think the wood-block print is a portrait of your mother on her journey.

Perhaps this version is as likely as any other. What had your mother been expecting or hoping for? What must she have thought after leaving the bustling Tokyo suburb where she was raised to arrive in the high desert with its arid sandy expanses dotted with sage, prickly pear, and cholla—all spread out beneath the pink-tinged granite splendor of the Sandia Mountains?

2. Land of (Dis)Enchantment

When does the Land of Enchantment become less than enchanting for your mother? Her later, more candid, accounts would seem to indicate disenchantment set in soon after her arrival.

Is it when your father, who she claims had promised to cook for her, only seems able to cook scrambled eggs and chicken, and she's "tricked" into having to take over the cooking?

Is it the first time he goes hunting with his brother and leaves her at home alone where, without the protection of a man, she's convinced she will be *murdered*?

Is it when she realizes your father wants nothing more than to be a cowboy, to work at your American grandparents' ranch in Wyoming, which your grandfather, a former petroleum engineer, purchased following an early retirement?

Is it when she realizes that in your father's fantasy ranch life, he envisions his wife as a *helpmeet*, someone who's willing to *pitch in*—the way your American grandmother bottle-feeds the orphaned lambs at all hours of the night during lambing season?

Is it when she learns, and is outraged by the fact that, your father sends money from his small pittance as a graduate teaching assistant to his parents because the ranch is struggling?

Is it when his mother, your American grandmother, a former

schoolteacher with a college degree, advises your Japanese mother not to have any children because mixed-race babies are *ugly*?

3. Famous Slumps

When he's in his eighties, your father confesses to you that he thinks your mother's mentally ill. He suggests she might be bipolar.

This isn't news to you, although you think her symptoms resemble something more along the lines of toxic narcissism and borderline personality disorder. What comes as a shock, though, is your father's admission because previously he's always seemed to be in a state of complete denial about your mother's mental health.

Your father says he first noticed something wrong early on in their marriage. They were in downtown Albuquerque, and your mother didn't like where your father had parked the car. As your father describes it, your mother became completely incandescent with rage and she had an explosion. That's the word he uses: *explosion.*

You understand this is a story in which your father is, among other things, looking for sympathy, but you have very little to give. You wonder why, if your father *knew* your mother was mentally ill, he didn't try to help her by seeking appropriate medical care. You wonder why, if your father *knew* your mother was mentally ill, he never stepped in to protect you from her emotional cruelty, her unpredictable and abusive rages.

But your father, too, suffers from dark bleak moods—what your mother refers to as his *famous slumps*—punctuated by scary, volatile bursts of anger.

Oftentimes, you felt like a lightning rod for your parents' misplaced rage toward one another.

4. Ground Zero

You're in Taos, New Mexico, for an artist's residency. You're also trying to *get your head on straight.* That your head isn't on straight feels hideously apparent to you and has for some time, but mostly you just try to get by, keep your head above water, *hit your marks*. The state of your head not being on straight feels like a rusted metal lid whose threads are stripped from too much grinding. Now the lid won't properly screw back onto the jar. It is always *askew*.

Still, though, the news is frequently terrible. You think maybe there are good reasons for your threads being stripped: *Roe v. Wade* overturned by the Supreme Court, Russians shelling the Zaporizhzhia nuclear power plant in Ukraine, fire and floods as climate change unravels the planet's ecosystems, Salman Rushdie stabbed at a Chautauqua Institution literary event. Soon, contaminated water from the Fukushima Daiichi Plant will be released into the ocean.

On your first night in Taos, a coyote pads through the grove of trees outside your writing window at dusk. One afternoon, a skunk softly ripples by then pauses to stare intently at you. You think of Robert Lowell's skunk in "Skunk Hour," with her "white stripes, moonstruck eyes' red fire / under the chalk-dry and spar spire of the Trinitarian Church." The skunk who "jabs her wedge-head in a cup / of sour cream, drops her ostrich tail, / and will not scare."

Instead, you feel more like Elizabeth Bishop's "glistening" armadillo fleeing the scene of the burning mountain—"rose-flecked, head down, tail down." Unlike the skunk outside who will not scare, you're already scared. You think of your unwillingness to leave the shell of your domicile. How, since the advent of COVID, a debilitating social anxiety makes you want to, like the armadillo, seal yourself up into a watertight ball and hide.

During the final days of your residency, you keep waking to the sounds of the couple who live on the other side of the back fence viciously arguing. You leave the windows open at night to keep the casita cool, and around 7:00 a.m., you hear them screaming and swearing at one another. Eventually, the man jumps into what sounds like a large truck and, with much gunning and revving of the engine, roars out of the neighborhood while the woman continues to yell after him.

Your head's not screwed on straight. You're having trouble getting your mind to stay present within your body. You're having trouble leaving your casita. The work you've doing at your artist's residency is raw, confessional, emotionally difficult. You imagine yourself sending in engineered robots to decontaminate the melted-down nuclear reactor of your childhood.

Here, in New Mexico, you feel as if you're at Ground Zero of your parents' marriage.

5. Midcentury Modern

Your sweetheart flies in to Albuquerque, and you spend a long weekend in Santa Fe together. You take long drives to soak in the shifting play of light and clouds on the Sangre de Cristo Mountain Range. You drive to Lamy. You drive to Camel Rock. One afternoon you drive past Bandelier, past White Rock, up the stunningly beautiful but vertigo-inducing hairpin curves of the Pajarito Plateau to Los Alamos, where you visit the Bradbury Science Museum.

Los Alamos is the site of the Manhattan Project, where J. Robert Oppenheimer, along with a world-class team of international physicists, oversaw the creation of the atomic bomb. They jokingly referred to it as "The Gadget." Under the code name Trinity, the first nuclear bomb was detonated on June 16, 1945. The Trinity test site's located 251 miles away from Los Alamos at the White Sands Missile Range, in New Mexico's La Jornada del Muerto desert. La Jornada del Muerto translates loosely from the Spanish as "Route of the Dead Man."

The site was chosen because it was deemed to be "sparsely populated." It reminds you of the sites selected for the concentration camps where Japanese Americans were incarcerated during World War II: Tule Lake, California; Minidoka, Idaho; Manzanar, California; Topaz, Utah; Jerome, Arkansas; Heart Mountain, Wyoming; Poston, Arizona; Granada, Colorado; and Rohwer, Arkansas. There are even four detention facilities and camps in New Mexico located in Santa Fe, Fort Stanton, Lordsburg, and the Old Raton Ranch in Lincoln County.

Despite this illusion of "sparse population," however, the top-secret site for the Manhattan Project in Los Alamos displaced and disrupted several local Pueblo communities, most notably the San Ildefonso Pueblo. Not to mention that approximately thirty-eight thousand people, including various Native American tribes and pueblos, lived within a sixty-mile radius of the Trinity test site and were neither informed of nor warned about the detonation. People within a ten-mile radius who unexpectedly witnessed the flash suffered temporary blindness. The mushroom cloud from the explosion extended 7.5 miles up into the atmosphere, and radioactive ash from the plume sifted down onto local surfaces for days after the blast. Several hours after the detonation, it began to rain. Crops, water, milk, and livestock were all most likely contaminated. Hundreds, and possibly even thousands, of "Trinity downwinders" died from radiation-induced cancer and disease. Even now, cancer rates in New Mexico counties near Trinity are four to eight times higher than the national rate.

At the Bradbury Science Museum, you're shocked by the replicas of Little Boy and Fat Man: the colorful displays, the cozy nicknames, how shockingly *small* the bombs are. One of the current ongoing missions at Los Alamos is for scientists to preserve and protect the nuclear stockpile, but still . . . what happens when natural disasters caused by climate change—fire, flood, earthquake—inevitably collide with weapons of mass destruction?

It strikes you that in 1955, your mother goes from frying pan to fire with a kind of unironic ease. She leaves Japan, the first and only site of deliberate nuclear holocaust, only to arrive in New Mexico, literally hours away from where the atomic bomb was created and test detonated.

Like a chain reaction, like the falling of dominoes, the dropping of Little Boy and Fat Man on Hiroshima and Nagasaki brings a swift end to the war, followed by the American occupation of Japan. Then the American troops continue to remain in Japan for the Korean War. Your father is drafted into the army and stationed in the personnel office at Camp Ojima in Ota City, where he meets your mother. Fission. Acceleration. The super collision of charged particles. They elope on the tenth anniversary of Hiroshima and begin their marriage in New Mexico. Ten years later you are born—a child of the Atomic Age.

Re-Membering

An Archaeological Catalogue

> I remember, in dime stores, "bronze" horses in varying sizes from small to quite large, with keychain-like reins—JOE BRAINARD, from *I Remember*

You are not allowed to touch the bronze horses with "keychain-like reins," which reside on the bookshelf next to your father's desk. One of the horses has a missing front leg. You worry that maybe at some point you *touched* the horse and broke off its leg. The horse reminds you of the straw horse that was missing a front leg who was friends with a tin soldier with a—was it a missing arm?—from a vintage picture book that you carefully study at length. You live in constant fear of amputation. Your father tells you about a hitchhiker whose kidnapper and rapist chopped off both of her hands. When you pull a hangnail, he says that your finger is going to have to be amputated and *How will you like them apples?*

The house has never really felt like your house or your home. It has always been an existence of don't touch, don't look, don't open, don't go in there. Now you are lonely and you go in all the rooms, open all of the drawers and closets and tins and boxes, look at every single item, and touch all of the things.

You remember the bent tin cup used to rinse off soap water in the bathtub, ringed with a parade of zoo animals circling the misshaped rim. The semicircle etched on the wall next to the towel rack left by the daily scrape of its round battered mouth.

The yellow Stylaire step stool with two nested steps that cleverly lift out and unfold. Your mother likes to call this the "high chair" for some reason. When you're on the swim team, your father uses the chair as a diving block. He holds up a pretend start gun and makes you practice competitive start dives onto your parents' mattress.

The small black clutch with a turn-lock clasp and a Netsuke of a woman's face dangling from the side on a small yellow cord. Inside, it contains a haphazardly folded "Personal History Statement," dated September 1, 1955—presumably part of the paperwork filled out by your mother when she applied for the job as a typist at Camp Ojima, the American occupation camp where she met your father. It feels eerily similar to the four-page "Personal History Statement" Japanese Americans were required to fill out prior to the Japanese American internment during World War II.

14A. list *all* organizations, societies, clubs and associations, *past* or *present*, together with addresses, in which you have held membership, give complete names and addresses in both japanese and romaji, include dates of membership.

14B. are you or any of your family present or former members of the communist party or any communist organization? if so, *state circumstances.*

You remember the name Sucrets, which sounds like "secrets." Inside the navy blue and pale yellow tins, the surprise of bobby pins, sewing needles, paper clips, or a house key wrapped in aluminum foil—buried beneath rocks by the back door in case of lockouts. The original foil-wrapped cough lozenges a long-gone memory. But you love conjuring up the word, *lozenge*, which seems shimmery and beautiful. There is earnest ad copy printed on the inside of the tins, interspersed with oddly deployed single quotation marks and *shoutycaps*:

SPEEDY RELIEF OF MINOR THROAT IRRITATIONS: "SUCRETS." Lozenges are not only pleasant to the taste—they contain soothing, analgesic and antiseptic medication. That is why they speedily relieve minor throat irritations associated with coughs and colds. They are ideal for relieving "smoker's throat" and for easing throat discomfort following tonsillectomies. "SUCRETS" Lozenges are manufactured by the makers of "S.T.37" Antiseptic Solution. ANTISEPTIC THROAT LOZENGES; TESTED FOR GERMICIDAL ACTIVITY

A cracked yellow diaper pail with a used Cup-o-Soup Styrofoam container jammed upside-down onto the top of the lid to act as a makeshift handle. It is filled with used toilet paper. At one point your mother apparently forbids the flushing of toilet paper down the toilet because the plumber has to be called in once a year to clear the pipes. Your father says it's because of tree roots. The plumber says it's because of tree roots. Your mother unilaterally decides, nonetheless, that the problem is caused by your father flushing toilet paper down the toilet and that the expense of having the plumber come once a year to clear out the pipes is *bankruptcy making.*

The magenta plastic box decorated with a Mod graphic of a woman with Liza Minelli hair and *Laugh-In* eyelashes your mother buys downtown, seeking a kind of transformation. The sides fold open to reveal an uncanny Styrofoam head, wearing a black wig. Your mother never actually wears the wig outside the house. You remember the night because it is Christmas Eve, and your parents have taken you to Woolworths to see Santa Claus. You notice there is adhesive tape on the side of his beard. You remember thinking it suspect. Years later, your bald father will wear the wig to a Halloween party, along with a quilted vest sewn by your mother in the style of a Gunne Sax vest. He is posing as a "rock star." He thinks he is being hilarious. His point seems to be rock stars, with their hair and their vests, are—to his mind—effeminate. He frequently likes to point out men who he suspects are effeminate, sometimes on the basis of their published poems or stories. He refers to these men as being "wet."

The American Way of Housekeeping: the most-used book in your mother's kitchen cabinet of cookbooks. A book so worn the cover has become detached—pages yellowed and loose, interspersed with bits of folded notebook paper with your mother's faded grocery lists. Published in 1948 by the Far Eastern Literary Agency & Publishing House, Inc., the dedication page cryptically reads: "The American Way of Housekeeping of the Women of the Occupation by the Women of the Occupation for the Women of the Occupation." Subsequent editions have been amended to read: "The American Way of Housekeeping of the Ladies of the American Community by the Ladies of the American Community for the Ladies of the American Community and Their Japanese Friends." Primarily intended as a how-to book for Japanese women in service to American families during the post–World War II occupation, or for the Japanese wives of American GIs, the book is written in both English and Japanese by American women residing in Japan and every page spews a blithe torrent of internalized misogyny and externalized racism:

> Your mistress will instruct you regarding the use of the sweeper or vacuum cleaner. Be sure to follow her instructions exactly. A vacuum cleaner should have gentle care. Do not bounce it or drop it. When you plug it in, do so very carefully. If, when doing so you remove a lamp plug, be sure to put it back. Do not attempt to pick up lumps of mud, twigs, leaves or large bits of food with a vacuum cleaner. Such things clog the tubes of the machine. When you have finished with the vacuum cleaner, remove the plug of the vacuum cleaner very carefully. Do not jerk it out.

You remember the pungently sour and chemical smell of Wite-Out. The tiny brush, like applying fingernail polish. The slightly grayish-blue undertone of it. In your childhood bedroom, bottle after bottle of dried-out Wite-Out with crusted-out insides like rotted nuts. You chart the progression of your father's cognitive decline after his stroke through the use of Wite-Out. The stroke you find out about years later, after it's already too late. The stroke your mother treats by putting him to bed and giving him a cold washcloth for his head. The painstakingly obsessive check registers rendered increasingly illegible by glopped-on coats of Wite-Out before they stop altogether. The page after page of Wite-Out splotched paper in which he tries to retype a review of his first novel, again and again. The Wite-Out crusted notecard that reads: *thanks for meeting you if you need to hear from me anything our number is* ___-__________.

You remember the Eberhard Faber Van Dyke typewriter eraser you love to sneak out of your father's desk drawer and scrutinize on rare occasions when both of your parents are out of the house. The hard pink gummy circle of it pierced with an embossed silver hub attached to a Mohawk brush bristle with which to brush away the eraser crumbs. The delight of recognizing this beloved object writ large decades later, rounding a street corner in Las Vegas, as a giant sculpture by Claes Oldenburg rendered in fiberglass and painted stainless steel.

The fake plastic owl with a red stopper plug like the bottom of a piggy bank that your parents put in the Nanking cherry bushes to deter the squirrels from scuttling across the rooftop. You remember the day they look out the kitchen window and become outraged when they discover a squirrel clinging to the owl's back, frantically *humping* it. The owl decoy is then brought inside to gather dust and balefully survey the dining room with its intense golden eyes from atop the china cabinet. There's a real owl that lives outside now. You hear its soft breathy hooting at night. In summertime, it scoops up baby rabbits from the front lawn—their bone-chilling screams flinting off a scrape of sparks from your 2:00 a.m. spine. The squirrel, or perhaps a descendant of the squirrel, now nested in your chimney, cantankerously rattling the chimney flue damper. Sometimes you can hear it softly sneezing.

The empty red Mrs. Fields cookie tin with a paper towel on the bottom and a note with a drawing of a squiggly face, tongue stuck out, that reads *Hi!* Did someone gift your parents the tin of cookies? Or did your mother buy the empty tin at one of the garage sales she obsessively scoured every weekend? The handwriting looks like your mother's. Did she leave the note for your father to find?

A turquoise-and-cream Star-Flyte brand heating pad with sleek, Jetsons-esque atomic age font and intriguingly liberal use of ellipses in the copy: *"3 Positive Fixed Heats – Low . . . . Medium . . . . High" "Soothing Comforting Heat for Aches and Pains . . . at the click of a switch!" "Directions . . . Read Carefully"*

It's a house that's filled with empty boxes and hollow containers, the original contents disappeared like meat from a lobster's claw. It's a house of cast-off shells, shed snake skins.

Like the molted mayfly skins that delicately cling to the window screens in early summer—their translucent, three-tailed, cuticular exoskeletons casting small shadows—until the wind cools, becoming gusty before rain, and blows them all away.

Drive(n)

1. Sybille Canyon

The drive through Sybille Canyon from Laramie to Rapid City a kind of glorious unribboning. A satiny tension unspooled around hairpin feldspar curves into a calm sense of presence. You feel attentive, yet relaxed. It's a drive that's stimulating, but without the white-knuckled hypervigilance required of a tricky and vertiginous mountain pass. The light is buttery, hot, and bright—a strong golden summer light that's sweetening as it ripens into fall. The shadows of fast-moving clouds dapple the fields with a shifting tumble of amorphous shapes.

2. Not Your Mother's/Father's Anxiety

For you, any departure has, as its prequel, an intense bout of anxiety. You like to say you're *bad at transitions*, which is true. Before any event, trip, or outing—no matter how *keenly anticipated*, no matter how much you *know* you'll enjoy it once you're *there*—your primary thought during the days before you're scheduled to leave is how much you emphatically *don't want to go*.

Yet it seems you're always departing, always on the move, always going somewhere *else*. Much less so since COVID, of course, but still.

You ameliorate the inevitable surge of anxiety through careful planning. You try to anticipate all the things that might go wrong. You think about how you'll handle various contingencies. It's not about control. It's about feeling like you can trust yourself not to *freak the fuck out* if (and when) things go awry. People sometimes say you're good in a crisis, but really? You've just spent a lot of time in your head obsessively gaming shit out in advance.

This anxiety about travel isn't even really your own, but it's so foundational, so instinctive, it seems impossible not to *feel* it. Your parents frequently harangued you as you were growing up for not exhibiting an appropriate level of *worry*: worry about money, worry about controlling what people were saying about you behind your back, worry about failing to triple- or quadruple-check the locks before leaving the house. By the time you were an adult, travel was one of the things for which they felt you exhibited a pathologically careless disregard. And it's not that you weren't anxious. You just weren't anxious about the things your parents *wanted* you to be anxious *about*. You remember feeling overwhelmed with anxiety as early as age four or five. Like a too-full glass of water, there was always/already so much anxiety that taking on any *additional* anxiety would have meant spilling over into . . . what?

3. Surfing the Liminal

Every time you exit and accelerate onto the interstate, though, anxiety immediately dissipates into exhilaration. Instead of being *driven* you are *driving*. Your to-do lists, deadlines, and obligations temporarily lift away. You're in control of your own destination. It feels like freedom.

Having left one place without having arrived at another, you feel yourself slipping into a liminal space that's all movement, possibility, transgression, flux. You could change your mind, change directions, if you really wanted. You could go *anywhere*. You love the feeling of being held in suspension between two possibilities,

Schrödinger's catlike, gliding along a fluid spectrum between home and not home, (t)here and not (t)here, dead and not dead.

4. The Driver's Seat

Your parents' sense of who was and wasn't allowed to drive was generously laced with misogyny. Your mother had her own car, but it mostly sat unused in the garage. Your father was always the driver, your mother always the one being driven. During your senior year of high school, when you were occasionally allowed to drive yourself to school, you were forbidden to drive past the city limits. Your father never taught you how to navigate the interstate. Yet during your sophomore year of college, you were allowed to ride back to Indiana University with a boy you'd been seeing, also a sophomore, who was returning from a summer internship in New Mexico.

Even well into your middle age, your parents spammed you with phone calls every time you drove out of town for a professional obligation: an out-of-town reading, a residency, a conference. They berated you for your stupidity and yelled at you about your imminent and inevitable demise on the highway! Sometimes you think you've been *hardwired* to feel as if you're suicidally courting death and disaster every time you leave town.

You stopped taking these calls after your parents phoned you over and over again the night before you were scheduled to drive out of Yellowstone Park—saying they'd read about a recall notice on brakes for your make and model of Jeep. You told them your car had been serviced before the trip, but still, they wouldn't stop calling. You were already a little bit tense because the return trip out of the east entrance involved driving on the outside edge of a narrow two lane steeply perched on the side of a mountain with dizzying curves and sheer drop-offs.

The vertigo set in as you neared the summit of Sylvan Pass, and by the time you were able to stop for a moment on the shallow shelf of a pullout to catch your breath, you were having a full-blown panic attack. The swoon you were feeling was twofold: the vertiginous hairpins of the mountain pass seemed almost unbearable in tandem with the surreal beauty of Yellowstone Lake—the pearled-milk reflection of clouds curdling and lustering the water. All of it ringed by the unholy sapphire blue of the Absaroka Range. Beauty intensified by terror. As you hyperventilated in your car, your options seemed limited: (1) just plunge off the side of the mountain to your death and get it over with; (2) call 911 and ask to be airlifted away by emergency helicopter. With shaking hands, you eventually called your sweetheart and asked him to help "talk you down."

5. Rest Stop

On the drive through Sybille Canyon from Laramie to Rapid City you usually stop twice. Once at Dwyer Rest Stop, near Wheatland, Wyoming, and then again at the TA Express Travel Center near Hot Springs, South Dakota, where US Highways 385, 18, and 79 intersect.

At the Dwyer Rest Stop there's an incredible view of Laramie Peak: iconic, looming, serenely blue hued. One afternoon you see a small fast lizard scurry across asphalt into the decorative bushes on the other side of the restrooms.

6. Chicken Out

When you were younger, your antidote to anxiety was sometimes to simply hurl yourself into reckless behaviors with a kind of self-destructive abandon. As you continue to age, you're still trying to find the balance between anxiety and negligence. Fine-tuning this spectrum's tricky, and the fulcrum tips so easily into either a kind of querulous reclusiveness or finding yourself enmeshed in a sketchy situation that feels unsafe, uncomfortable, *regretful.*

You decide, for example, to drive to an artist's residency in Oysterville, Washington. The scenery will be beautiful, you say. It will be an adventure, you say. But as the trip approaches, you begin to fret. You read up on grades, road conditions, possible highway closures. You discover that Oregon has a law requiring tire chains in inclement weather. You worry that by early November, on the return drive, the weather will have turned. In the end, you *chicken out* and book a flight to Portland.

You're unsure if you've made a sensible decision, or if you've spinelessly acquiesced to an anxiety that's not even yours. It reminds you of the microwave saga. For years, you listened to your parents complain about how *expensive* it was to heat up the whole oven just to reheat leftovers. For years, you volunteered to buy them a microwave, only to have them say a microwave was too complicated to figure out, too *dangerous*.

At one point, they asked you to use the internet to book them a hotel for an out-of-town trip. When they received the room confirmation you'd printed out and sent to them via snail mail, they became excited because the room came with a microwave! So you wrote down step-by-step instructions for how to use the microwave, then sent those along to them by snail mail as well. Later, when you checked in to see if they'd enjoyed using the microwave and asked if they'd like you to send them one for Christmas, your mother said: "We chicken out! Too dangerous!" Then she added: "We decide you shouldn't use it either."

And that's the thing about the fulcrum. You don't want to end up like your parents—too frightened to even *try* using a hotel microwave. But you also don't want to find yourself stuck in a miserable situation of your own making—unhappily white-knuckling your way through treacherous and unfamiliar mountain passes with poor road conditions in inclement weather.

7. Fireball!

The morning you drive to the Laramie Regional Airport for your flight to Portland, you see, on the horizon, just outside the city limits, what you can only describe as a *deconstructed rainbow*. It's sort of a low hanging blob, or cloud, but in a pretty blur of rainbow colors with an oil spill's shape and sheen. Like a spilled bowl of melted rainbow sherbet. You can't decide if it makes you uneasy or happy.

Despite a recent rise in COVID cases, you're one of only three people in the airport who's masked. Prior to opening up the security screening area, the gate agent announces that while there are currently no masking or vaccine requirements, passengers are asked to be *respectful* of other people's choices. Some travelers may have health issues, he says, and other travelers may have loved ones with health issues. The subtext clearly seems to be one in which the unmasked are being asked to be respectful of the masked. You wonder what being respectful of someone else's choice to wear a mask entails. Not tearing their masks off? Not harassing or assaulting them?

There's an unmasked woman sitting several seats to your right in the waiting area. You recognize her as being the woman who, when she first entered the airport, sniffed her armpit and exclaimed, "I still stink of Fireball!" During the announcement about respect, she vehemently shakes her head and begins muttering angrily. She glares at you, affixing you with full-on stink eye: "Nope," she says, under her breath. "Not gonna do it. Hell, no."

8. Ocean View-ing

In retrospect, you frequently feel *chagrined* by the amount of anxiety you sometimes push through to accomplish the most banal, or ordinary, of acts. But then again, chagrin's so quickly replaced by joy when you find yourself on the open road in a rental car, having successfully untangled yourself from metropolitan Portland traffic.

Because now you're driving along the greenly scenic Oregon coast until you arrive on the beach in Seaside—overlooked by the craggy Tillamook Head promontory—where you are soothed by the frothed slap and churn of the tide.

Then you are driving across the lower Columbia River into Washington, suspended like a small silver raindrop on a spider's web, high in the air upon the beautiful Astoria-Megler Bridge—spanning 4.1 miles, the longest continuous truss bridge in North America.

And then you're making your way up the Long Beach Peninsula, past the towns of Ilwaco, Long Beach, and Ocean View, all the way into Oysterville: where there are clams nestled into the sand waiting for you at low tide, where there are many delicious oysters to eat, where there are giant banana slugs to befriend and admire, where there's a strange rooster that inexplicably crows a howling wobble of a cock-a-doodle-doo all afternoon long, and a cabin in quiet green where you will write and write and write all month and there is no *don't* and there is no *can't* and there is no *shouldn't* and you aren't feeling driven, you are in the driver's seat, and you are free, free, free.

Left Hands of Darkness

1. Nail Stuck Up

Your mother used to tell you that as a baby you clearly presented as left-handed. She says you instinctively reached out for things with your left hand. That you clearly gave preferential treatment to your left hand. She then likes to boast that she "corrected" you from being left-handed by tying down your left hand so you couldn't use it. Eventually you were forced to acclimate by using your right hand instead.

From your mother's point of view, this is a story in which she's cleverly saved you from a lifetime of marked deviance: a lifetime of having to use left-handed scissors, a lifetime of having to sit in left-handed desks. Perhaps she's thinking of the Japanese saying *deru kugi wa utareru*—the nail that sticks up gets pounded down.

From your point of view, though, this is a story that reveals how, in your mother's eyes, even as a baby, you were always/already "wrong," unacceptable, in need of punitive corrections.

As a young adult, you obsessively researched Japanese culture in the hopes of being able to understand, or translate, your mother's troubling or painful behaviors toward you. Was it so that you could take responsibility for a failure of comprehension on *your* part, some sort of cross-cultural misunderstanding *you* were guilty of? Because of course wasn't that less painful than the alternatives?

When you research *deru kugi wa utareru* you learn that to be a nail stuck up not only refers to deviant or nonconformist behavior but also refers to behavior that excels in ways that attract undue attention or potential jealousy. How do you reconcile this with your mother's refusal to help you blend in more comfortably with your classmates, even though you were relentlessly bullied? How do you reconcile this with your mother's insistence that you always had to get the highest score, the best grade, and win every single competition in order not to be a complete and utter failure in her eyes?

What would you be like, who could you have been, if you weren't a baby who was stymied by having one hand forcibly tied down?

2. The Devil's Hand

As a young, aspiring concert pianist in Laramie, Wyoming, you occasionally took lessons from a retired concert pianist, pedagogue, and composer, Allan Arthur Willman. Mr. Willman, as you called him, had studied in Paris with composer Nadia Boulanger, under the recommendation of legendary pianist Ignacy Jan Paderewski.

Sometimes Mr. Willman would ostentatiously call up the music school at the University of Wyoming and reclaim his former studio from the chair of the piano department for your lessons. Other times, you would play for him at his house. You remember books and art, a harpsichord placed against one wall, a Steinway grand centered in the living room. His sweaters always gave off the spicy stench of cigars.

You have a very specific memory of Mr. Willman teaching you the names of the hands in French and Italian one afternoon, as he explained the notations for hand crossovers on a piano score.

m.d.—main droite, French for the right hand, indicating that a passage was to be played by the right hand
m.g.—main gauche, French for the left hand, indicating that a passage was to be played by the left hand

m.d.—mano destra, Italian for the right hand, indicating that a passage was to be played by the right hand
m.s.—mano sinistra, Italian for the left hand, indicating that a passage was to be played by the left hand

When he said "mano sinistra," he dramatically lowered his voice and waggled his bushy eyebrows at you. Something cracked open and was illuminated, like the inside of a geode. You think maybe this was one of the first times that the connotative life of a word, of language, felt so explicitly revealed.

3. Maladroit

When you're a sophomore in high school, you're unexpectedly shoved so hard by a boy in the band room after school that your right wrist is fractured as you fall backward onto the floor. You lie to your parents, say that you slipped and fell going down a flight of stairs. Why do you lie? Somehow, you're convinced that you'll be blamed, that you'll be punished for having been shoved by a boy. Why is this, though? Is it because they blamed you for having been sexually assaulted by an eighteen-year-old when you were only nine? Do you feel they'll say you did something stupid to invite this anger, this roughness? You can't remember now if there was joking around or some kind of adolescent roughhousing that preceded the incident, but you do remember being surprised by the force, the intense hostility, at the moment of being shoved. As soon as you land on the floor you know you've been hurt even though you pretend that you're not. You never tell anyone. But it's not to protect the boy; it's to protect yourself. *Why?*

During high school you practice six to eight hours of piano a day. Obsessively. Maniacally. In part, you do it because you're bored. Even though you were allowed to take college classes at the university lab school you attended throughout junior high, you're no longer allowed to take college classes in high school. In part, it feels like a form of escape, a way out of Laramie. And in this, you're not entirely wrong. Now that you know yourself better, the memory of this obsessive practicing feels a lot like an SSB, a self-soothing behavior—a way to quell anxiety, to escape into daydream, to dissociate.

Your parents are irritated by your clumsiness, but the lie still feels like the better option at the time. You suspect your instincts to lie were right. But *why*?

The wrist bone that's fractured doesn't receive much blood flow, so you're in a cast for two months, all your spring piano competitions canceled, and now it's your right hand that operates within a constraint.

Your specialty, as a pianist, is French Impressionism, so you decide to learn Maurice Ravel's Concert for the Left Hand. This tour de force of left-handed virtuosity was commissioned from Ravel by pianist Paul Wittgenstein (older brother of philosopher Ludwig Wittgenstein) in 1929 and completed in 1930. Wittgenstein, a concert pianist, was shot in the right elbow by Russian soldiers in Galicia during World War I, leading to most of his right arm having to be amputated. The hospital where he was recuperating was then captured by Russians, and he served time in a camp for prisoners of war. Following his release, he commissioned various composers, including Benjamin Britten, Richard Strauss, and Sergei Prokofiev, for piano work written exclusively for the left hand. The most famous of the commissions ended up being Ravel's Concerto for the Left Hand with its glittery, jazz-inflected arpeggios and sweetly pensive melodies.

4. Linguistic Hegemonies

Right

1 : RIGHTEOUS, UPRIGHT

2 : being in accordance with what is just, good, or proper
// *right* conduct

3 : conforming to facts or truth : CORRECT
// the *right* answer

4 : SUITABLE, APPROPRIATE

// the *right* man for the job

5 : STRAIGHT

// a *right* line

6 : GENUINE, REAL

Left

1a : of, relating to, situated on, or being the side of the body in which the heart is mostly located

// her *left* leg

4 *often capitalized*

a : those professing views usually characterized by desire to reform or overthrow the established order especially in politics and usually advocating change in the name of the greater freedom or well-being of the common man

b : a radical as distinguished from a conservative position

Phrases containing left: "left a bad taste in my mouth" "left him at the altar" "two left feet" "left to rot in jail/prison"

Dexterous

1 : mentally adroit and skillful : CLEVER

// her *dexterous* handling of the crisis

2 : done with mental or physical skill, quickness, or grace: done with dexterity:

ARTFUL

// a *dexterous* maneuver

3 : skillful and competent with the hands

// a *dexterous* surgeon

Sinister

1 : singularly evil or productive of evil

2 : accompanied by or leading to disaster

3 : presaging ill fortune or trouble

4a : of, relating to, or situated to the left or on the left side of something

especially : being or relating to the side of a heraldic shield at the left of the person bearing it

b : of ill omen by reason of being on the left

Adroit

: having or showing skill, cleverness, or resourcefulness in handling situations

// an *adroit* leader

// *adroit* maneuvers

Gauche

1a : lacking social experience or grace

also : not tactful : CRUDE

// it would be *gauche* to mention the subject

b : crudely made or done

// a *gauche* turn of phrase

5. Nonbinary

In any binary opposition, one term exists as the privileged term, and the other term exists as its inverse, for the purpose of marking it as deviant, denigrated, Other. For the purposes of designating center from margin.

These doorways are linguistically coded and foundationally baked in.

To draw attention to the hierarchies of the binary is to inevitably draw cries of fragility, victimization, as well as dangerous backlash from those who occupy the space of privilege. If one refuses to admit to occupying the center, then one can also deny the justice of being asked to de-center.

Perhaps the greatest transgression against privilege is to ambidextrously glide along a fluid spectrum, for then you are a moving target: to be racially ambiguous, queer, trans, or nonbinary means that you do not acknowledge the place that has been arbitrarily assigned to you. It means you do not agree to the labels that sort margin from center. It means that you are "illegible" to the terms of empire, to the terms of power.

6. Ambi = Both

Deru kugi wa utareru.

Even if your mother was trying to keep you from being the nail that got pounded down when she tied down your left hand, it still meant you had to fight with one hand tied behind your back. Maybe this led to certain virtuosities, but it also created certain deficiencies.

Your life has been a long episode of failure to distinguish yourself in the ways your mother wanted you to distinguish yourself and sticking out in ways your mother insisted brought her shame. And yes, you have been pounded down.

But in truth, it was your mother who pounded you down the most. She pounded you down and she pounded you down and she pounded you down to the point that there are days, even as an adult, where you do not feel capable of even leaving the house.

You are still untying your left hand.

The hand that's closest to your heart.

Your hand of darkness.

Falling

The phone rings in the middle of the night. Your mother's fallen out of bed again. There are no marks and she doesn't seem to have hit her head. The staff at the assisted living center say they will put her on a twenty-four-hour watch.

◎

There is something skittery in the chimney. At night you hear it descend with scratchy claws. Once in a while, the sound of a small soft sneeze falls out of the fireplace flue.

◎

The phone rings in the middle of the night. Your mother's been shouting in her room, where she's fallen out of bed again. There are no marks and she doesn't seem to have hit her head. The staff at the assisted living center say they will put her on a twenty-four-hour watch.

◎

The coyote's howl a rising spiral of sound in the night that tornadoes up in the dark, then falls back down into silence.

◎

You remember, from your childhood, a book of sheet music with a green-and-blue striped cover—popular songs from the 1950s. Your mother can't play the piano, but she fakes it, repeatedly chunking out the same chord as accompaniment. "Falling in love again," she moodily sings again and again in a quavery, out-of-key soprano.

◎

The cicadas' song building in call and response, from tree to tree, until a circular wall of sound is built, blotting out the sky, and darkening, like a bruise, before suddenly falling off.

◎

The phone rings in the middle of the night. Your mother's crawled into the hallway after falling out of bed again. There are no marks and she doesn't seem to have hit her head. The staff at the assisted living center say they will put her on a twenty-four-hour watch.

◎

In the evening, two ants struggle to drag the body of a dead moth up the window screen. For a time, the moth seems to levitate awkwardly, jerkily—as if reanimated—before it's dropped. The ants climb back down the window screen and the moth eerily levitates again, before it's dropped again and falls.

◎

The phone rings in the very early hours of the morning. Your mother's fallen out of bed again. There is pain in her wrist, and she cannot move it. The paramedics are called and she's taken to the hospital. An X-ray reveals a wrist fracture. At the hospital, she removes the temporary cast, becomes agitated and combative. She starts hitting the nurses. Eventually, she's taken back to the assisted living center, where she falls asleep for the rest of the day.

◎

Sometimes you see the owl, who likes to perch in the Russian olive tree, plummet from its perch at dusk. At night, you hear the screams of baby rabbits.

◎

Once, your father fell down a flight of stairs and through a plate glass door, carrying a mimeograph machine donated to the local AAU swim team from a downtown law office. The plate glass slices right through him, missing the vital organs but leaving a foot-long fishhook of a scar down his back. Your mother decides that he is dying. The first night he's in the hospital, she talks about going back to Japan when your father dies. She says she might not be able to take you with her because you don't speak Japanese.

◎

In his poem, "[Lana Turner has collapsed!]," Frank O'Hara writes: "I have been to lots of parties / and acted perfectly disgraceful / but I never actually collapsed / oh Lana Turner we love you get up"

◎

The phone rings in the middle of the night. Your mother's fallen out of bed again. The nurse is worried that your mother might have hit her head against the nightstand. There's a bruise on the side of her temple. The nurse says that your mother seems alert and that she doesn't appear to have a concussion, although it's difficult to tell because of the Alzheimer's and because your mother no longer speaks English. The staff at the assisted living center will keep her on a twenty-four-hour watch.

◎

A skunk crosses the yard in front of your window with its loping walk full of flourishes that is a kind of cursive. Later on at night, a cloud of skunk smell rises then falls, with the settling dusk.

◎

When your father fell to the bathroom floor of the assisted living facility, he struck his head, causing a catastrophic brain bleed. The chronology of events goes something like this: Your father lies on the bathroom floor, with the door open, while your mother fumes in the next room, as she does every day before lunch. She's mad because she claims he's always putting face cream on his face. She says he's trying to look younger to impress the girls. She says that he's snitched all her money and given it to his new girlfriend. By the time staff arrive to take your parents to lunch, your father is unresponsive. Around 2:00 a.m. the next morning, the hospital calls to tell you that he's gone.

◎

A millipede falls on the bathroom floor—from where? from where did it fall?—with a soft little plop.

◎

In Iowa, windmills slice the mist. One blade at a time disappears into the sky and takes turns pretending to be a ghost, before falling back down into materiality.

◎

The phone rings in the middle of the night. Your mother's fallen out of bed again. Apparently, her chest hurts and there's bruising on her left side. There's also pain when she tries to raise her left arm. The nurse is worried she might have injured her ribs. The paramedics are called and she's taken to the hospital, where X-rays reveal four cracked ribs and a small pleural effusion. The emergency room doctor decides to take your mother off the blood thinner, Eliquis, which has been prescribed to your mother to help prevent stroke due to her atrial fibrillation. The doctor explains that a cerebral hemorrhage from the repetitive falling is now a statistically higher risk.

◎

In early summer, armadas of mayflies come and line the window screens of the Wyoming house with their sway-backed bodies and cellophane wings. Soon they molt, and their translucent husks cling on like tenacious ghosts, until a summer storm loosens their grip and they fall.

◎

The phone rings in the early afternoon. Your mother, who's just been discharged from the hospital after having fallen and cracked her ribs, has fallen again on her way to lunch, losing consciousness. When the paramedics arrive, she's in atrial fibrillation. At the hospital, they do another round of bloodwork and X-rays. They discover a urinary tract infection. Your mother's prescribed an antibiotic and released back to the assisted living facility.

◎

When your father was alive, he used to keep a little black cassette player next to his desk. The kind with the black push-button keys. There's a plastic sack full of cassette tapes that he likes to listen to. His favorite is Linda Ronstadt. Sometimes you hear her cover of Patsy Cline's "I Fall to Pieces" floating out from behind the shut door of his bedroom.

◎

Meanwhile, on the other side of the house, maybe your mother is listlessly plinking at the piano, singing "Autumn Leaves," in the melancholy style of the Frank Sinatra cover: the lyrics describing drifting leaves by the window and missing a beloved most in autumn, when the leaves begin to fall.

◎

In the fall, leaves lose their chlorophyll, stop reflecting green light, and their veins shut down. Other chemicals, enzymes, and hormones surface. Scar tissue forms at the base of the leaf—a layer of cells called the abscission layer—and the connection between leaf and tree weakens. Eventually, gravity, or the wind, detaches the leaf and it falls.

◎

Abscission: you wonder if this is what happened all the times your mother told you there was no longer any connection and you were no longer her family.

◎

Abscission: you wonder if this is anything like the scarring of plaque in your mother's brain, the falling away of her memories, her language, her self.

◎

The phone rings in the middle of the night . . .

Colony Collapse

1. Post

Late 2022 and petulant billionaire blowhard Elon Musk's acquisition of Twitter's just been reluctantly finalized. The platform's all stirred up and buzzing. Accounts are archived, locked down, deactivated. Poets and writers begin a weird migration in which they Goldilocks their way through various social media apps: first Mastodon, then Post, then Hive. Eventually, most seem to entropically settle back into Twitter again. But there are periodic flurries of movement whenever the platform becomes subject to particularly stupid corporate decisions or whenever there's a surge of alarming signs of technological decline or instability: Spoutible. Threads. Bluesky.

You've been uneasily perched atop the landslides of the hoarding-infested ruin of your childhood home, trying to carve out small clean spaces in which to keep your socks and underwear, a couple of coffee mugs, your favorite cooking pan. You've been more or less living out of a suitcase for nearly a year. (A one-semester visiting professorship, ten weeks at one artist residency, four weeks at another. In-between times spent attempting to unhoard your childhood home in Laramie.) You've been feeling especially peripatetic, restless, disenfranchised. You've recently become obsessed with TikTok, and although too shy to post, you're secretly riveted to the scrolling panoply of capybaras, cats, recipes, and quick snippets of therapy.

2. Hive

Around the time that literary Twitter's anxiously swarming back and forth from Mastodon to Post to Hive, the TikTok algorithm magically proffers you a video from *texasbeeworks*, run by professional beekeeper Erika Thompson—a woman who documents bee rescues. She locates colonies precariously situated in garbage bins, backyard compost bins, abandoned washers, and even inside an abandoned toilet tank. She also homes disenfranchised swarms clustering along the underside of tables, in construction scaffolding, or beneath patio umbrellas. Thompson coaxes the colonies and swarms into new, clean hives that she pulls out from the back of her truck. In a typical bee rescue, Thompson first transfers over any extant honeycomb, to "save the bees' hard work." In many videos Thompson, who doesn't wear a veil or gloves, gently scoops up bees with her bare hands as she carefully initiates the move. When she's able to locate the queen bee, she places her into a clear plastic clip that can be pinned into the new hive. At this point, and with some smoke, the rest of the bees will voluntarily migrate over. Thompson's narration is quiet, low-pitched, fast-paced, and ASMR-ishly soothing. She concludes each video by softly intoning, "And it's another great day of saving the bees!"

In truth, you're a sucker for any and all videos regarding the transport of living things out of harm's way into safety: sloths and tortoises gently carried off busy highways and deposited into trees and greenery on the side of the road, a dog stuck in mud at the bottom of an arroyo lifted out with ropes, a family of geese relocated off the third-floor ledge of the National Geographic Headquarters in Washington, D.C.

The National Geographic goose rescue is a particularly elaborate operation in which city wildlife experts are called in once the goslings are ready to jump off the concrete ledge and fledge. Two of the goslings easily jump down, flapping themselves to safety, but the third gosling's unsure. When the timid gosling reluctantly jumps, it's awkward and ungainly, and there's a scary gust of wind as it hurtles toward asphalt. But disaster's averted when one of the wildlife rescuers deftly catches the gosling in a net. There's a burst of applause from anxious onlookers! Then the goslings are placed in a carrier to ensure that the parents will follow, and the entire goose family's ceremoniously escorted by city wildlife through over a mile of busy D.C. city traffic—until they arrive at their new home at Constitution Gardens, which has a large pond.

You find something deeply reassuring about the gentleness, attentiveness, and care in these animal transport narratives in a time that's so frequently characterized by *unrepentant assholery*. The viral videos provide a quick hit of dopamine in the midst of ongoing feelings of despair over environmental collapse.

3. Mastodon

You'd been trying to aspire to a similar model of gentleness, attentiveness, and care when you were forced to relocate your declining parents into assisted living. How the situation felt similarly dire: your mother falling asleep with the stove burners still on; your father unable to stand on his own and repeatedly urinating in their shared bed; your parents refusing to allow the social workers dispatched for wellness checks by their medical care providers into the house. Your mother, the queen bee, gently maneuvered into a transparent clip and pinned into the new hive—so that your father, in order to join her, finally agreed to be transported to the assisted living center from the nursing home where he'd been undergoing rehab. It's not that you expected gratitude, or even thanks, but there was something about the speed with which your parents turned on you—casting you as an avaricious cartoon villain, with sinister and self-serving mustachio-twirling intentions. Because single-handedly orchestrating this move while working full time, less than a year out from cancer surgery, had been a huge disruption to your own life—a serious sacrifice of time and energy and resources on your part—and being castigated for it was, frankly, *demoralizing*.

4. Spoutible

But so much of dealing with your parents' decline has felt like the daily news—an exhausting seesaw between the downright cataclysmic and the unnervingly absurd. In the midst of all this nauseating sloshing, these tempests threatening to wreck *all* the teapots, you find yourself trying to make the most of small hopeful progressions, trying to cling to rare little life buoys of sanity. For you, one of these life buoys was the announcement, in early 2023, that a vaccine to protect honeybees from American foulbrood had been developed by a biotech company in Georgia and was conditionally approved by the U.S. Department of Agriculture.

Foulbrood, though less deadly to honeybees than varroa mites, seemed like such a gratifyingly repulsive target for the first bee vaccine. Highly contagious, foulbrood's easily transmitted from hive to hive. Caused by the *Paenibacillus* bacterium, foulbrood causes honeybee larvae to turn a disturbing dark brown. Hives infected with foulbrood apparently give off a pungent smell of decay and rot, hence the name. Prior to the development of the vaccine, contagion could only be stopped through burning down entire apiaries, as well as any equipment that had come in to contact with infected bees. While antibiotic treatments were also a possibility for dealing with foulbrood, studies have shown that antibiotics are harmful to honeybees' long-term health and development.

In the Pick Your Dystopia bingo card, Extinction of Pollinators ranks highly among your personal Four Horsemen of the Ecocide—situated squarely alongside Unpotable Water, Unbreathable Air, and Pandemics. So the swell of gleeful rejoicing in certain corners of social media in response to the news of the bee vaccine made perfect sense to you. In fact, you were heartened that so many people might be charmed by the news of a bee vaccine. You, yourself, were exceedingly charmed by the news of a bee vaccine!

5. Threads

As the COVID pandemic continues to malinger, you've been wondering if there's been some sort of ecological tipping point in which zoonotic novel viruses, caused by damaged and dwindling ecosystems, will continue to manifest, proliferate, and surge. That we've now officially entered the Age of Pandemics. And if not the Age of Pandemics, it seems to be, at the very least, a kind of Age of *Contagion*. Anything can *go viral* now—including disinformation, lies, and conspiracy theories. You can't help but feel as if there's something distinctly pathogenic and profoundly contagious going on with the QAnon believers, The Great Replacement Theorists, the Flat Earthers, and the COVID is a Hoax-ers. It gives you the same *squicky*, lifting-up-a-rock-to-discover-something-squirmy-and-upsetting feeling you felt when you discovered the shocking avalanche of mail-out materials from the NRA and the five loaded handguns stashed in your childhood bedroom at your parents' house. The colony seems ill with a kind of collective mental foulbrood. Like *folie á deux* gone viral.

The challenge in developing the bee vaccine, it turns out, has to do with the fact that insects don't have antibodies, which are the proteins within an immune system that both recognize and fight off bacteria and viruses. However, once scientists realized that even without antibodies, an insect could acquire immunity, and genetically pass it down to their offspring, they were able to create immunity within a honeybee queen through feeding her royal jelly laced with the vaccine—created from dead *Paenibacillus* bacterium. When the vaccine makes its way into the queen bee's ovaries, immunity is conferred to all her hatching larvae.

You think of what's been passed down from your own mother: the allergies to bees, wasps, spiders, mosquitos; the allergies to wool and horsehair; the high blood pressure; the extreme anxiety. You think of epigenetic trauma. Could the narcissism, the sudden rages, the behavior that presented like textbook borderline personality disorder have possibly been circumvented or at least ameliorated? What changes in your mother's early circumstances might have conferred immunity: Not having to grow up in the midst of bombings and war during her childhood in Japan? Your Japanese grandmother not dying in childbirth when your mother was only fourteen?

You consider the smooth gliding prophylaxis evoked by the sound of the word *immunity*, how the way the word *sounds* creates a kind of cognitive dissonance with the officiously administrative or clinical shields of its legal and medical meanings. You are, and always have been, someone who is too porous, too easily saturated. You lack in antibodies. You desire immunity. You wish you could be more immune *to* and immune *from* your mother.

6. Bluesky

In one of her TikTok videos, Erika Thompson finds a dilapidated red suitcase on the side of the road containing an old hive of bees. The bees have no food or no brood, but she says the bees are very gentle, unless faced with a direct threat. When a wasp flies into the suitcase and immediately disappears, Thompson remarks that the bees "defended their colony and eliminated the wasp." When you do a little bit of research to discover exactly how a hive deals with foreign intruders such as wasps, you're fascinated to learn that bees can heat their abdomens up to over one hundred degrees. They cluster around a threat, forming what is known as a "heat ball," that cooks and suffocates the intruder to death. Thompson loads up the suitcase into the back of her truck and takes it home with her, where the bees voluntarily move themselves into the hive that she proffers to them in her backyard. Thompson says they recognize that it's a better place for them to live. The queen independently walks herself into the new hive, without needing to be transferred into the special clip. The video concludes: "And it's another great day of saving the bees!"

Sometimes you wonder how much of your current state of feeling geographically displaced, or unsettled, has to do with feeling relationally and emotionally unsettled by the merciless disintegrations of your parents' physical and cognitive decline. Your father's death. Your mother—who used to be larger than life in both her charisma and her cruelty—slowly fading away from Alzheimer's. Are you living out of a suitcase from necessity, or are you running away from something—trying to *out-abandon* pending abandonment? When you inevitably become an orphan, will you finally be able to settle down and find a home for yourself, or will you become even *more* unsettled—a balloon floating away on a let-go string?

Thanksgiving

All the first graders are wearing hats cut out from construction paper and assembled with Elmer's glue. Half the class wears a black Pilgrim's hat garnished with a yellow buckle. The other half wears a headband affixed with a single feather—quill and vanes crudely drawn in with black crayon. Because you're biracial, you're told you must wear a headband with a feather. It's not like you particularly *want* to be a Pilgrim. But somehow, being explicitly gatekept from the possibility of even being *allowed* to pantomime a Pilgrim in a construction paper hat still rankles. It reveals to you the ways in which the privileged position in the binary is clearly *Pilgrim*. It reveals to you the ways in which Pilgrim is synonymous with *whiteness*. And just like that, the foundational pulleys and gears of white supremacy are made apparent to you.

Desks have been pushed together to form a makeshift table. There's a pumpkin pie feast. It's a performative reenactment of Manifest Destiny and nation making—a synecdoche formed and maintained by the crudest and simplest representative symbols.

◎

Thanksgiving's a holiday that's always felt *lonely* to you. Everything quiet. Everything closed. Only the three of you—your mother, your father, and you—eating turkey in your pajamas. Never any relatives. Never any friends. If your mother's in one of her rare good moods, she hypervigilantly eagle-eyes your plates, speculates out loud about which item of food each of you will eat first: turkey? stuffing? the can-shaped circle of cranberry sauce your father slices into careful rounds with a butter knife? She's pegged you as someone who *always* eats the stuffing first, and although you don't necessarily believe this to be true, you've learned to just eat the thing she claims you're going to eat first so she can triumphantly claim, *I told you so!* You don't want to make her mad.

◎

You remember a rare Thanksgiving in which your family's invited to dinner at the home of one of your father's former mentors. It's stressful and weird. Your mother's irritated, but it's decided there's no possible way to decline, so the invitation's accepted with a kind of martyred resignation. Your mother insists everyone must dress formally (in *suits*!) and multiple outfits are selected, tried on, vetted in advance. It turns into an exhausting ordeal. Afterward, during the debriefing, the entire meal's mercilessly critiqued. The *stinginess* of only bringing small slices of breast meat to the table on a platter! The cranberry sauce, which was made from scratch, was *sour*! The pumpkin pie was *store bought*! They wanted to drink *sherry* before the meal like *alcoholics*!

◎

You do not *intend* to projectile vomit all over the first grade elementary school pumpkin pie feast. In fact, you do not have any *inkling whatsoever* that you are about to projectile vomit all over the pumpkin pie feast, until it suddenly happens.

The story of how you projectile vomited all over the first grade pumpkin pie feast becomes the salacious and hilarious gossip of your elementary school for several weeks. And what remains isn't the scariness or pain or discomfort of having become violently ill but the embarrassment, the shame, of vomiting in public.

◎

Every year, your father carves the turkey at the kitchen table on the bright yellow-gold Fiesta Ware platter used to serve up the bird. The Fiesta Ware platter was handed down from your American grandparents along with some other leftover pieces. You remember the color so well. It still glows faintly in your memory: something in between a marigold yellow or a goldenrod. It's the color of moons made from cheese in children's books, and so you used to think it was fabricated from an actual piece of moonrock. As an adult, you learn that Fiesta Ware manufactured between 1936 and 1972 used uranium to create some of the colored glazes. Sources recommend using a Geiger counter to determine if your Fiesta Ware is radioactive.

Several days after you projectile vomited on the first grade Thanksgiving feast, there's an accident. As you father carves the Thanksgiving turkey, the bird slides, the knife slips. The platter goes clattering down to the kitchen floor and breaks in two. Your mother's sadness over the platter is, of course, understandable. After all, you were also enamored with its hot marigold glow. What's truly unsettling, though, is the way in which she's instantly transported into an incandescent rage. She spends the afternoon screaming at your father, screaming at you, then afterward she's inconsolable. Thanksgiving is ruined.

In retrospect, so many holidays were ruined by your mother's emotional weather. You remember vividly the urgent anxiety with which you remote-controlled your father into purchasing Christmas gifts you hoped might please your mother. How, if she was disappointed by the gift, she'd casually and contemptuously toss it onto the floor. How the mood for the rest of the day would go sour. You remember how, when you were first told as a young adult that you were no longer welcome home for Christmas, your mother insisted it was because you always caused drama.

◎

You are not, and have never been, a *good vomiter*. In part, it's that you find the inside-outness of vomiting somewhat traumatizing, but it's also that, as a child, you were never able to correctly identify feeling *vomity* in advance.

Once, when you were a toddler, you threw up in your parents' bed, and after that, you were never allowed to climb into their bed again. Your mother was furious. For years, she bitterly referenced this incident as something terrible that had happened *to her*, something terrible that you had done *to her*.

In general, it's always been difficult for you to identify when you are feeling ill, when you are experiencing pain.

◎

When you're an undergraduate in college, your parents say it's too expensive, too inconvenient, to fly you home for the weeks of Thanksgiving and spring break. The university cafeterias are closed, so they mail a box of Ramen noodles and canned food to your dorm. When all the other students leave for the week, you're the only person left, and you rattle around in the empty dorm like a weird ghost.

Your parents lavishly praise themselves for all the trouble and expense they've gone to in sending you the box full of Ramen noodles and canned food. *Who else going to send their daughter such nice box of food?* your mother demands. *Nobody!* You're thankful because you're told to be thankful. You're thankful because you're forbidden to take a part-time job, so it's not like you have any pocket money, anyway, so what else can you be? You're thankful because you don't have any other choice.

It's decades before you recognize this as a kind of gaslighting.

◎

When you're sent home midafternoon after projectile vomiting on the pumpkin pie feast at school, your mother's angry, in the way she always becomes angry when you're sick or injured—insisting that it's all your fault. That you must have done something stupid to cause your own illness, as if illness is a form of *disobedience* on your part—a deliberate act to create extra work and inconvenience for your mother. She's angry that you've *embarrassed* her by projectile vomiting on the pumpkin pie feast at school. She calls you a *liar* because when you'd come home for lunch that day you'd been glassy-eyed and feverish, but when she asked if you felt sick, you said you didn't feel sick.

In truth, you didn't *think* you felt sick. Is it that you have a bodily awareness problem? Or do you not trust your own pains, feelings, and sensations because whenever you report them, you're told you're being a *hypo-psycho*? How do you know if something is "real" or if something is "all in your head"?

◎

More and more, you wonder what designates "home" for someone who's never truly felt "at home"? What does it really mean to be "home for the holidays"?

But still, you remember a certain kind of sweetness: homemade pumpkin pie under a dollop of Cool Whip on a metal TV tray in front of the Macy's Thanksgiving Day Parade. The delightful, wobbly procession of beloved giant balloons flickering in grainy black and white.

In 1971, two days after you projectile vomited all over the first grade Thanksgiving feast, you're watching the Macy's Thanksgiving Day Parade, eating Saltine crackers instead of pumpkin pie, oblivious to the fact there's been a balloon disaster the night before due to extreme weather: Smokey the Bear's hat requires extensive repair, Happy Dragon's head is severely damaged, and Snoopy ends up wrapped around the cab of the helium truck. All the balloons grounded due to high winds. You're unaware of this behind-the-scenes carnage because there's a tricky sleight of hand in which representation triumphs over the real, and footage of the balloons from the 1970 Macy's Thanksgiving Day parade is being aired on the television instead.

Several hours later, the Thanksgiving platter's broken and Thanksgiving's officially ruined. Because you're only in first grade, and because your secret name is Scapegoat, you believe that, somehow, you're to blame. You become convinced you've somehow ruined Thanksgiving by projectile vomiting all over the first grade Thanksgiving feast. There have been glimmerings all along that you might have the power for mass destruction and *ruination*, that you're an assassin of happiness, a wrecker of future holidays, and this is the Thanksgiving in which this belief becomes baked in.

(And yes. You understand the difference between what one feels and what is intellectually and psychologically true. But still.)

Decades later, and you're "home for the holidays." Your mother's locked in a memory care ward, and your father's ashes are sitting in his kitchen chair where the Thanksgiving platter was broken. You putter half-heartedly through a house clotted with your ghosts and a half-century's worth of hoarding, feeling like some obsessive Miss Havisham, armed with a Geiger counter for trauma. The hot yellow, possibly radioactive, glued-together piece of Fiesta Ware simmers in the kitchen cabinets beneath an avalanche of used Blue Bonnet margarine cups (*everything's better with Blue Bonnet on it!*), used aluminum foil, used napkins, used grimy rubber bands that have lost their elasticity, and expired food.

The Wyoming wind gusts and gusts. The parade balloons of late Empire shrivel and deflate.

Dreaming in the Fog

It's late summer in Homer, Alaska. Land of the midnight sun. Even though it's the coldest and rainiest summer on record in over fifteen years, the days when mist burns away to reveal the white-frosted peaks of the Chigmit Mountain Range across the glassy surfaces of Cook Inlet are astonishingly beautiful. It's a hallucinatory, surreal kind of beauty. Sometimes you're almost glad for the silky gray cloud cover, the mornings blurred in veils of fog—both for the ways in which joy feels even *more* joyful when the mountains become visible again in their blazing blue ferocity, as well as for the relief from the intensity of so much beauty, so much light. It's the kind of intensity that feels as if it might precariously topple over into mania with the slightest nudge.

On sunlit days, a slow and reluctant sunset spills golden light through your cabin windows well past midnight, dipping down into a kind of twilight in between 1:00 a.m. and 3:00 a.m., before resuming its yellow siren call of light. In the very early hours of these bright mornings, you have potent, vivid dreams.

You dream you're in your childhood home in Laramie, Wyoming. You climb on top of the kitchen counter, then gingerly clamber atop the ancient, wheezing refrigerator, which wobbles. When you're on top of the refrigerator, you crawl through the wooden cupboards above the refrigerator, which you understand is a kind of portal, or a wormhole, to access the basement, which isn't really the basement, but is something more along the lines of a pocket that exists outside of time.

In this basement, you find your mother. She's lucid, her English restored, and she's uncharacteristically cheerful. Because you're never sure what you're going to get in any encounter with your mother, you approach her with trepidation. Even though it's precarious to climb on top of the kitchen counter and onto the wobbly refrigerator, and even though it's uncomfortable wedging yourself through the wormhole in the cupboards above the refrigerator, you keep going back through, again and again, to visit your mother in the basement that's not really the basement. You're worried your mother might be lonely and bored down there, all by herself. You try to bring little gifts with you, although the gifts end up being strange: a spatula, a rod of bamboo, a soft ribbon. The gifts are, as in real life, inadequate. You feel guilty and sad for keeping your mother stashed in the basement that's not really a basement that can only be accessed via the wormhole above the refrigerator. But you understand there's no safe way for you to pull your mother out—that if you try to remove her, the Alzheimer's, the physical frailty, the complete loss of English in exchange for her native Japanese will return.

◎

In the morning, fog sometimes crawls out of the inlet and sheeps its way through the trees, breaking off into soft woolly tufts before it evaporates away.

Several mornings after you dream about the wormhole over the refrigerator, your mother's assisted living center calls. Your mother's had a fall. Nothing appears to be broken, there are no bruises, and she doesn't seem to have hit her head. Your mother's falls come in surges and cycles—sometimes a cluster of multiple falls during a matter of weeks, then no falls for months at a time. Usually the falls happen at night, so you sleep next to your phone, perpetually clenched for emergency. Depending on the severity of the fall, your mother sometimes ends up needing to be admitted to the hospital. During the last cluster of falls in the spring, your mother hit her head hard enough that the paramedics had to be called. At the hospital, she became cyanotic, then tested positive for COVID. Sometimes when she's at the hospital, your disoriented mother becomes agitated, combative, and starts hitting the nursing staff.

◎

You dream you're in your parents' basement. You're removing clothes from the clothesline. There's a washer in the basement, but there's never been a dryer. As you remove clothes from the clothesline, some of the oppressive junk and clutter—the house is hoarded up to the gills—begins to disappear a little bit in the area around the clothesline where you're working. As the clothesline becomes lighter and lighter, it starts to move in an automated loop, presumably to help the clothes on the line dry more quickly. You perceive this to be something your father's engineered. At the moment, you feel in awe of your father's creativity and genius, though when you wake up, you realize that installing a dryer in the basement would have been a much more sensible and less labor-intensive solution. You think about how this encompasses so many things about your father: the ways in which he could make an unnecessarily grueling and tedious ordeal out of the simplest and most basic of tasks; how his career as an emerging and well-published novelist came to a baffling halt after the publication of his second novel; how on several occasions he angrily blamed you for his stalled-out career as a novelist; how he seemed to be in complete denial of the fact that it was, instead, your mother who sucked all of the oxygen out of any room, who required caretaking, constant attention, the entirety of his emotional bandwidth; how he publicly professed pride over your own literary achievements, yet privately encouraged and subscribed to the family mythology in which he was the genius, the writer with *actual* talent, while you were the hack who got lucky, coasting on his coattails—the one who was always doing it embarrassingly, definitively *wrong*.

In the dream, you search for the source of the automation, which you believe to be located somewhere on the basement ceiling, so that you can turn it off. You're worried about wasting electricity. You're worried about fires. The clothesline continues to loop around and loop around and loop around, and you think to yourself that your father's dead. You feel a fury of grief inside you. In the dream you realize this emotion far exceeds the sad muffled confusion you usually feel when you think about your father's death.

◎

Some mornings, there are Rubenesque banks of clouds odalisqueing on the horizon, obscuring the mountains—slow to rise, snoozing half the day away.

Following your mother's most recent morning fall, the nurse who calls you tells you, in a careful and measured way, that "for some reason, we're not exactly sure why" your mother was wearing another resident's shoes. The other resident's shoes were not only much too big for your mother, but one of the shoes had a significant lift to accommodate the resident's disability, causing your mother to fall.

You're not sure if the nurse really *doesn't* know why your mother was wearing another resident's shoes, or if the nurse is kindly trying to spare you the details, but you feel as if you know *exactly* what's happened. Your mother probably saw the other resident's shoes, identified them as her own after deciding the other resident had "snitched" her shoes. (*Sono kutsu wa watashi no mono desu!*) You feel pretty sure your mother probably took the shoes right off the other resident's feet. You know this because it's something that's happened before in various iterations. Your mother's father, your Japanese grandfather, used to own a bespoke shoe store in Japan, and your mother's obsessed with shoes. You know this because your mother likes to tell you that CNAs have been "snitching" her shoes from her room when she's eating, and she also accuses *you*, with particular vitriol, of having "snitched" her shoes. Sometimes you compare shoes with her, to show her you don't even wear the same size, to demonstrate how your feet are too large to wear her shoes, and she tries to take away the shoes you have on, saying you're a liar, and the shoes you're wearing are really *her* shoes that you've "snitched" from her.

◎

You dream your mother's back in her house again, sitting next to a tall blonde woman on the sofa. Your mother asks the woman if she knows her friends, Taisetsu and Santa Claus? The woman's long arm is wrapped around your mother's shoulders, and your mother's laughing. She seems happy. You have an uncomfortable, uneasy feeling, though, because you know Taisetsu and Santa Claus aren't real. They're Pokémon. Taisetsu is a green, elfish frog-shaped Pokémon, who has a Pokémon friend named Santa Claus. In the dream you feel confusion. Is the Pokémon's name Taisetsu, or is it *Kaisetsu*?

You also feel a distinct pang because the way your mother is with the other woman is the mother you've always wanted. Smiling, charming, affectionate, warm. Okay, maybe a little bit helpless. The broken wing raised high to disguise the gears of manipulation. One part of you knows this is the public mask your mother puts on, that later, in private, she will congratulate herself on how well she "buttered up" the other woman. But another part of you remains the child trapped alone in the house with your mother's terrifying, secret unmasked self: the child who's been made to understand that she *deserves* the terrifying, secret unmasked self; the child the mother threatens to throw away in the garbage for the garbage man to find—who'll be replaced with the garbage man's much-more-deserving daughter; the child who knows the funny, happy, smiling mother mask doesn't belong to her, will *never* belong to her. Even now, decades later, you feel the pang of jealousy when the public mask's conferred upon someone else. And why wouldn't it be? Of course, they're clearly more deserving. Look at them, sitting there with their arm around your mother. So kind and caring. No conflict. No ambivalence. Your mother basking in the glow of their attention. Look at them. Thin, tall, blonde, comfortable in their own skin. Why wouldn't your mother prefer them to you?

The woman, you realize, is partnered to one of your ex-lovers. You're sitting on the floor with him in the adjacent room. You're both laughing together a little sheepishly over the fact that your mother thinks the Pokémon Taisetsu and Santa Claus are real. (Or is it *Kaisetsu* and Santa Claus?) Together, you're looking at a large folding map. Periodically, you pull the map up in front of yourselves as a shield, so the other woman and your mother can't see, and you kiss. It's not really sexy kissage, nor is it romantic kissage. It's more like *sneaky* kissage. It feels like spin-the-bottle kissage. There's another man, someone you don't know, someone you don't recognize, in the room with you, sitting on the piano bench. From his higher angle of viewing, he coolly observes you kissing your ex-lover behind the large folding map.

◎

One morning, the fog slowly poofs up from the inlet like an overblown soufflé—overflowing all the way up to the top of the ridge, rising over the roof of your cabin. You see it moving in front of your window. It's like being inside of a cloud. It takes until the middle of the afternoon for it to clear.

In real life, this inability to tell the difference between technology and reality had been one of the ways in which you identified that your mother was in cognitive decline. How when you showed her your Pokémon Go game on your phone, she thought the Pokémon were real. How she thought Siri was a real person, and she'd angrily snap at you for not saying "thank you" to Siri. Or she'd become upset with you because she thought it was too late to "call" Siri and you'd wake Siri up. Or she'd berate you because she was sure you'd been stupidly tricked into having to pay Siri money every time you asked for help.

But in real life, Taisetsu (or is it *Kaisetsu*?) and Santa Claus aren't "real" Pokémon. In the dream, you *recognize* the name Taisetsu (or is it *Kaisetsu*?) as an actual Japanese word, but you can't remember what it means. When you look it up, you realize that you have, in fact, encountered the word "taisetsu" in Duolingo. It means "important, necessary, indispensable, beloved, precious, dear, cherished valuable." "Taisetsu no hito" is a person who's more important than anyone else. When you look up "kaisetsu," you discover that it means "explanation, commentary, expository, *uncomplimentary remarks*."

◎

You dream you're inside a store, something vaguely Walmart-y, and you're talking to one of your friends from elementary school. She reveals something about the trauma, the abuse, she was going through at home. You're shocked because it's an exact mirror of the trauma, the abuse, that you were going through at the same time but never disclosed to anyone. Your friend has appeared to you as the small child she was in elementary school. You're an adult, so you firmly hold her hand in yours because the Walmart's crowded and uncomfortably chaotic, and you don't want to lose track of her. At some point, you realize she's not actually your friend from elementary school and that you're holding the hand of your own young self.

Now you're outside the Walmart, and the street becomes the street in front of the university lab school you attended in fourth grade, which is the age of the child whose hand you're holding, and there's a parade. It's a graduation parade! People are wearing caps and gowns, but it's been disrupted by some sort of disaster. Maybe floods. Maybe fire. At some point, the hand of the child that you were slips out of your hand and she disappears into the pandemonium. To your horror, you realize the child you've just lost is no longer your young self but your elderly mother instead. You frantically run around, panic-stricken, searching. You ask random strangers if they've seen your mother. You tell them she has Alzheimer's, that you're *responsible* for her. A group of professors in caps and gowns say they might have seen her heading in the direction of the Fine Arts building. You fight your way through the smoke and the water and the frenzied masses of people and make your way toward the Fine Arts building. The tumult, confusion, and danger increases. You don't see your mother anywhere. You become afraid that she might actually, truly be gone.

◎

The fog's burned away, it's a hot, bright day, and you're in a taxicab with other writers, flushed with wine and food. The driver says he used to work for the whaling industry, hunting beluga whales. He says that if a dead whale fell through collapsing ice, *everything* was lost, and they'd have to "start all over again."

Suddenly, a moose appears out of the greenery on the side of the road next to the taxicab.

You realize it's your mother's birthday. Somehow, you've completely forgotten or repressed or blocked the date. Your mother is now ninety-two years old. You know your mother no longer remembers her birthday or even has much concept of what a birthday *is* any longer, and you can't decide if this nebulousness of selfhood, this delirium of vapor and mists, is a kind of horror movie fog or if it any way brings some sort of relief from the intensity of wants, disappointments, resentments.

The moose that's appeared next to the taxicab is a young moose. Male, with small, broad, velvety antlers. You've never been this close to a moose with actual antlers before. It's running right alongside your taxicab. Running and running. Running and running. Before it disappears back into the greenery.

Unshelled

Sometimes, when you're feeling some kind of way, you describe it as being like a mollusk without a shell. More often than not, it's about the acid reflux of trauma: an evocation of feeling vulnerable and raw to the point of distress, of the ways in which your hypervigilance and hypersensitivity frequently leave you overloaded, overwhelmed, overstimmed. It's a feeling of being all open wound when everything that surrounds you is salt.

The only thing to do for it, you've found, is to hide. To secrete your body into the safe shell of your apartment, let your consciousness retreat somewhere outside your body, and just wait for it to pass.

It's not what you would describe as a fugue state, per se, but it's nonetheless an abandonment, an absenting, a kind of disassociation from the body and its constant vulnerabilities: its illnesses, its pains, its chemical imbalances, its manufactured shames. It's as if the self retreats to a cartoon thought bubble above the body. Meta. Away. Safe.

You understand this is possibly an anachronistic coping mechanism, but lately, you've become increasingly aware this is also the same mental space in which you *write*. Was this something you discovered as a child, growing up in an abusive household? Your consciousness absenting a body that was always wrong, safe in a room behind a closed door, free to expand, wander, daydream, and play? The sovereignty of it. The escape of it.

It's the first time you've conceptualized this space as being multi-use. Like a time-share condo! And yes, it encompasses the multiple shades of *retreat*. Retreat as in to back away from immediate danger or violence. Retreat as in solace, replenishment, nourishment. Retreat like an artist's residency. Re-treat as in to give oneself a treat again.

You love this quiet, disembodied space where you're all thought. All dream. All possibility. As an introvert maybe this is where you're most comfortable? And even if this is the same space where your traumatized self absents itself to, it's also the space your best self fills with daydreaming, music, language. Something like Robert Duncan's "place of first permission" from his poem, "Often, I Am Permitted to Return to a Meadow."

You understand there's a contradiction here: of feeling violently and nonconsensually unshelled by trauma, as opposed to being able to lay down the aching burden of too much armor—the tricky mediations of too much shell. The common denominator, perhaps, lies in the state of vulnerability, rawness, openness. Which can be either a wound, or an aperture.

Maybe because you know what it's like to come *unshelled*, you're fascinated by different types of shelled organisms. Snails, hermit crabs, armadillos. When you Google the term "happy as a clam" to find out its origins, you discover that, like many clichés, it's been truncated from its full phrasing, which is "happy as a clam at high tide." Meaning that at high tide, clams are burrowed into their sandy shallows, safe from being wrested out by clam diggers and other natural predators. And so it's not even really so much a kind of *happiness* as it is a respite from feeling *preyed upon*, a period of time in which a clam can remain *unmolested*.

Lately, your time-share system seems to have completely broken down though. Too many clamoring, demanding, and wounded selves have retreated from the overwhelming din of the present moment and are occupying your mental sanctuary all at the same time, making it impossible for the writing self to think. The traumatized self curls into the space like an oversized fetus—systematically sucking all the oxygen from the room. Then there's the to-do-list self, who's absented the disaster zone of the body and retreated to higher ground to make sure the whole enterprise stays afloat from a safe distance. The to-do-list self who flips on like an emergency off-site generator and coolly extracts tasks from a body that miraculously continues to shamble about like some kind of automata. *You hit your marks*, you repeatedly keep telling yourself, as if this is some kind of achievement, as opposed to being the lowest possible bar.

And admittedly, it's been the *shittiest* of timelines. Several months after Trump takes office, you're diagnosed with cancer and undergo a complete hysterectomy, salpingo-oophorectomy, radical trachelectomy, and lymphadectomy. Eight weeks after your surgery, your mother, who's refused to speak to you for three years, who's said that you're no longer her daughter, calls to say your father has fallen and broken his hip, that he's in the hospital. She's alone in the house and helpless, so you go to Wyoming to take care of her and to make arrangements for your father's recovery. Shortly after your arrival, you discover that your father has had an undiagnosed stroke and is suffering from vascular dementia. When your father finally returns home from rehab later that fall, your parents systematically undo all of the caregiving, transportation, and assistive arrangements you've spent all summer setting up for them. Ultimately, your parents are identified as vulnerable, your father no longer competent, and so you must file for legal guardianship of your father and move your parents into assisted living.

You do all of this in a fog of intense, chronic pain as your severe spinal stenosis becomes increasingly debilitating. Every morning there are grueling hours of back spasms, and when you first wake, you can't walk upright. Searing electricities slice through your extremities, like hot knives through butter. Sometimes there's a numb gray static, like television fizz, signaling that your legs are about to disappear from beneath you. Every movement, every task, becomes a calculation around the mathematics of pain. Pain, too, can be a kind of unshelling—erasing the intellect and leaving the raw meat of the body exposed.

On New Year's Day of 2019, your father falls at the assisted living center, suffers a catastrophic cerebral hemorrhage, and dies. You return to Wyoming to take care of the legal and logistical issues and to be with your mother, whose cognition is rapidly deteriorating. When you take her to the doctor, it's confirmed that she has Alzheimer's. You file for legal guardianship for your mother and stay in Wyoming for as long as you are able, then return to South Dakota just in time to have spine surgery.

It takes almost a full year for you to finally start to find a kind of familiar equilibrium following your father's death and your recovery from surgery. You're in the midst of a hectic series of readings to support your most recent book in the spring of 2020, when, like the other shoe dropping, news of a novel coronavirus becomes increasingly insistent, then increasingly dire.

You think of what happens next as a kind of *volvation*: the ability to roll oneself up into a protective ball when scared and/or threatened by predators. Gigantic Madagascan pill millipedes (*Glomeris pustulata*); woodlice, also known as pill bugs (*Armadillidium vulgare*); four-toed hedgehogs (*Atelerix albiventris*); and La Plata three-ringed armadillos (*Tolypeutes matacus*) all practice volvation.

You love the word volvation. And you're delighted, in particular, by the photos of three-ringed armadillos folding themselves up into watertight balls, a clever origami, heads and tails neatly tucked in, like a feat of engineering ingenuity. In your conceptualization of volvation, it's not simply a physical defense mechanism but a psychological defense mechanism as well. *Sample sentence*: In the spring of 2020, you volvate and neatly disassociate. Who knows where you've gone? Like a Japanese puzzle box. You imagine fiddling with the sliding pieces, the secret drawers, the patterned unlockings of the self. But you stubbornly refuse to crack back open again.

And why would you? It's a timeline checkered with psychological landmines and interconnected triggers. Having to preside over the late-stage wreckage of an abusive family not only raises personal remembrances of lack of safety, a complete lack of bodily autonomy, but these resurfacing vulnerabilities intersect with the atrocities of the contemporary moment. It's the *nonconsensuality* of it all. The refusals to wear a mask to prevent the transmission of COVID. The refusals to get vaccinated to prevent the transmission of COVID. The incessant gun violence, the bodies riddled with bullets. The ubiquity of rape with impunity and without accountability. The plundering of natural resources. These are the penetrative violences of rape culture. These are the extractive violences of empire.

And to take in all of this awfulness while remaining fully present seems like the most hideous kind of *rawdoggery*. So you seal yourself up and let the tiny, needling stressors ping dull little sparks of anxiety against your armor while you keep dealing with what's in front of you: the work, the overcommitments, the guardianship of your declining mother. You try to repress the things that aren't within your control, and you play a relentless game of whack-a-mole while the world burns. But still, it's *so fucked up*. This gaslit pressure to continue on as if everything is normal. (Also nonconsensual! Also extractive!) You think that there's a toll, there *must* be a toll, in trying to survive a time that's so cataclysmic, so disruptive, without the ability to process, to grieve, to take a breath and acknowledge how changed everything is and must be.

Extroverts are always saying that shy people need to *come out of their shells*. Why? Why this wish for obligatory unshelling that makes one vulnerable to predation or consumption? It doesn't seem like a coincidence that clams are slang for dollars. That clams are considered something delicious to be stubbornly plundered from their shells, to be pried out of their bivalves gripped shut by surprisingly strong musculature. *Happy as a clam!*

Yet your survival as a writer depends upon a delicate balance of both *presence* and *absence*. You've always been extremely shy, extremely introverted, and the pandemic has heightened all of this to the point of intense social anxiety. As COVID restrictions loosen, and you try to forcibly pour the self back into the body, it's shocking! To fully inhabit one's own body again feels like an uncomfortable and unpleasant process of stuffing the self back into a too-small sack. Like wrestling a futon into a new cover. A grinding awareness of software and hardware. The awkwardness of face and interface. An overwhelming and overstimming sense of presence, of feeling much too raw in the present. Where have you been? Where did you *go*?

Your self is not the same. Your body is not the same. A rejoinery that's both awkward and difficult. You feel like the creepy spectacle of the hermit crab who's poured itself into an abandoned doll head, laboriously dragging it along the beach in the viral YouTube video.

You wonder if this painful (re)integration of (re)occupying your own body is somehow a microcosm of what it might mean to be fully present in and fully (re)integrate, as human beings, into an abandoned and failing planet?

The trick of it, it seems to you, is to somehow sort out the difference between *retreat* and *retreat*.

Unvolvation: Since COVID, it seems like you've been *in retreat*, but now you are *on retreat*. For ten weeks, you've been given the gift of an artist residency in Taos, New Mexico, in mountains and clouds. Sometimes a coyote pads through the trees outside your window at dusk.

There are still fires. There is still COVID. Mass shootings continue unabated. *Roe v. Wade* has been overturned. There are horrific, ongoing genocides in the Congo, Sudan, Myanmar, and Gaza. Your frail mother continues to fall in the middle of the night at her assisted living center, breaking parts of herself: a fractured wrist, cracked ribs. But you are trying to unclench. You are trying to recalibrate a balance between presence and absence, between shelled and unshelled, and this respite is everything—this defined space away from the everyday world, this borrowed shell that exists purely for your writing self. For now, it is high tide, and for now you are going to try to be as "happy" as a clam.

Acknowledgments

Versions of these essays have appeared in the following journals and anthologies:

A Mollusk without a Shell: Essays on Self-Care for Writers, (Julie Brooks Barbour and Mary Biddinger, eds.), University of Akron Press, 2024—“Unshelled”

Dear America: Letters of Hope, Habitat, Defiance, and Democracy (Simmons Buntin, Elizabeth Dodd, and Derek Sheffield, eds.), Trinity University Press, 2020—“Dear America / Dear Motherland: An Essay in Fractures”

New Ohio Review—“Hall of Mirrors”

South Dakota Review—“Sixteen Views of the Bourgeaus: An Homage (Minus Twenty) to Hokusai’s Thirty-Six Views of Mount Fuji,” “Ghost-Busting in Wickenburg: A Resurrection of Sorts,” “Derby Dreams,” “Loop-de-loop,” “Scourge,” “Writing Down the Bones,” “Home(r) Sweet Home(r),” “Meditations on an Emergency,” “The Wind Phone,” “Anhedonia in the Anthropocene,” “Homeward Bound,” “Five Loaded Handguns,” “Leftovers,” “The Unbearable Privilege of Breathing,” “Dream of a Two-Headed Turtle,” “Lost in Translation,” “Austere and Lonely Offices,” “My Sister’s Keeper: An Essay of Unbraiding,” “The Atomic Age,” “Re-Membering: An Archaeological Catalogue,” “Drive(n),” “Left Hands of Darkness,” “Falling,” and “Thanksgiving”

Terrain.org—“Swarm” and “Colony Collapse”

West of 98: Living and Writing the New American West (Lynn Stegner and Russell Rowland, eds.), University of Texas Press, 2011—“Motherlands and Mother Tongues: Five Reflections on Language and Landscape”

I would also like to thank Storyknife, the Wurlitzer Foundation, Hedgebrook, Willapa Bay AiR, the Women’s International Studies Center at Acequia Madre

House, the Brush Creek Foundation for the Arts, the Bunnell Street Arts Center, the South Dakota Arts Council, the Banff Centre for the Arts, the Kimmel Harding Nelson Center for the Arts, and the University of South Dakota, for the gifts of funding, time, space, and support without which this book would not be possible.